D0699033

t.f.h.

The Proper Care of
GOLDEN RETRIEVERS

TW-143

Overleaf: Golden Retriever litter photographed by Isabelle Francais.

Facing Page: A blooming obedience and field Golden puppy—this is China owned by the author.

The portrayal and discussion of canine pet products in this book are for instructive value only and do not necessarily constitute an endorsement by the author, publisher, or the owners of the dogs depicted in this book.

Photographers: Ashbey Photography, Martin Booth, Fox and Cook Photography, Isabelle Francais, Alan Mills, Alice Pantfoeder, Robert Pearcy, Judith Strom, Chuck Tatham, Karen Taylor, and Jerry Varva Photography.

© 1997 by T.F.H. Publications, Inc.

Distributed in the UNITED STATES to the Pet Trade by T.F.H. Publications, Inc., One T.F.H. Plaza, Neptune City, NJ 07753; distributed in the UNITED STATES to the Bookstore and Library Trade by National Book Network, Inc. 4720 Boston Way, Lanham MD 20706; in CANADA to the Pet Trade by H & L Pet Supplies Inc., 27 Kingston Crescent, Kitchener, Ontario N2B 2T6; Rolf C. Hagen Inc., 3225 Sartelon St. Laurent-Montreal Quebec H4R 1E8; in CANADA to the Book Trade by Vanwell Publishing Ltd., 1 Northrup Crescent, St. Catharines, Ontario L2M 6P5 ; in ENGLAND by T.F.H. Publications, PO Box 15, Waterlooville PO7 6BQ; in AUSTRALIA AND THE SOUTH PACIFIC by T.F.H. (Australia), Pty. Ltd., Box 149, Brookvale 2100 N.S.W., Australia; in NEW ZEALAND by Brooklands Aquarium Ltd. 5 McGiven Drive, New Plymouth, RD1 New Zealand; in Japan by T.F.H. Publications, Japan—Jiro Tsuda, 10-12-3 Ohjidai, Sakura, Chiba 285, Japan; in SOUTH AFRICA by Lopis (Pty) Ltd., P.O. Box 39127, Booysens, 2016, Johannesburg, South Africa. Published by T.F.H. Publications, Inc.
MANUFACTURED IN THE
UNITED STATES OF AMERICA
BY T.F.H. PUBLICATIONS, INC.

The Proper Care of
GOLDEN RETRIEVERS

Nona Kilgore Bauer

Silverado's Emmett UD earned a Dog World *award and a Gaines placement on his way to his UD. Owned and lovingly trained by Marsha Ross.*

Contents

High Times Straight as 'n Arrow CD, MH, WCX owned by the author.

History of the Golden Retriever

The Golden Retriever could easily be called "a dog for all seasons." Bursting with talent, energy and affection, the Golden is considered the ideal dog to hunt cover, compete with, or just live with and hug a lot. As testimony to its popularity, the Golden Retriever has ranked among the American Kennel Club's top ten most registered breeds since the mid-1980s. Generally considered the most beautiful of the five retriever breeds,

Beauty is as beauty does. This family of four proves that good-looking Golden Retrievers can also excel in the field. L to R: KC's Sparkle Plenty MH and her three Master Hunter daughters, China, Spirit, and Dazzle.

Ada, born 1871: The property of the Earl of Ilchester. She was the daughter of Lord Tweedmouth's original dog.

the Golden is also the youngest, dating back to 1868. For many years, a popular and colorful tale held that the original Golden descended from a troop of Russian dogs touring with a circus in Brighton, England. The dogs were Russian Trackers, beautiful and intelligent guardians of the sheep flocks in the bitter-cold Caucasus Mountains.

A charming tale, but a myth of unknown origin. In 1952 the Golden's true ancestry was published in *Country Life,* a British magazine, in an article written by the Sixth Earl of Ilchester. A writer and historian, he published his research on the kennel records of his great-uncle Lord Tweedmouth.

Lord Tweedmouth, formerly Sir Dudley Marjoriebanks, was the

Fourth Earl of Ilchester. His estate, Guisachan (pronounced *gooeesicun*, a Gaelic word for "place of firs") rested in the beautiful highlands of Inverness, Scotland, overlooking the Tweed River. In the true spirit of the English in the mid-1800s, Tweedmouth was an avid sportsman and hunter, with an ardent interest in waterfowling. This sporting interest throughout the country had created a demand for dogs rugged enough to endure arduous hunting conditions on land and in water, dogs who would also willingly deliver the game to hand. Most breeders of the day shared a common interest in producing such an animal.

In 1865 Lord Tweedmouth purchased a dog named Nous (the Greek word for wisdom) from a

Four Goldens immortalized from 1930s' England: Silence of Tone, Noranby Black-eyed Susan, Ch. Noranby Diana and Noranby Jane.

cobbler in Brighton who had received the animal as payment of a debt. Nous was out of a black Wavy-Coated Retriever (ancestors of today's Flat-Coated Retriever), and was the only "sport" (yellow, and thus not considered standard) in a

Ch. Elysian's Lil Leica Reprint UDT, MH, WCX, VCX (SDHF) owned by Jeanne von Barby.

litter of otherwise all black pups. Two years later Tweedmouth's cousin gave him a Tweed Water Spaniel named Belle. The Tweed Water Spaniel was a liver-colored spaniel native to the Tweed River area, liver being the term commonly used to describe all sandy, fawn and light tea-colored dogs. These spaniels were popularly used along the British seacoast for both sport and livelihood. They were hardy, ruggedly-built dogs noted for their courage and intelligence and ability to retrieve game under all conditions.

In 1868 Nous and Belle were bred and, as Tweedmouth had hoped, produced four bright and fuzzy yellow

This painting by Nina S. Langly (1934) graced the famous Hutchinson's Popular and Illustrated Dog Encyclopedia.

pups whom he promptly named Ada, Crocus, Primrose and Cowslip. Ada, Crocus and Primrose were given to friends and relatives, and Cowslip stayed home, destined to become the foundation of Lord Tweedmouth's continued efforts to produce a yellow retriever breed.

In 1873 Cowslip was bred to a second Tweed Water Spaniel; Tweedmouth kept a bitch puppy and named her Topsy. Topsy was mated in 1877 to Sambo, a Wavy-Coated Retriever, producing Zoe, who was later bred to Sweep, a descendant of Ada. Tweedmouth kept Zoe busy, breeding her later to Jack, a descendant of Cowslip and a Red Setter.

Linebreeding of this nature was uncommon at that time, but Tweedmouth was dedicated to his dream and continued to breed these dogs to each other, occasionally outcrossing to a Wavy-Coat or Tweed Water Spaniel to preserve the strength of the line, and always keeping only the yellow or golden pups for his stock. Other experimental crosses were made to the Bloodhound and Irish Setter. Later breedings to the yellow Labrador also can be found in the pedigrees of certain lines of English Golden Retrievers.

Tweedmouth contin-ued to give other yellow pups to close friends along the way, and in time three other notable lines (or kennels) arose. Two of these, Ingestre and Culham, occasionally outcrossed to a yellow Labrador. Lord Harcourt of Culham's great sires, Culham Brass and Culham Copper, are behind some of the great Golden lines of today. Ingestre and Culham eventually registered with the Kennel Club of England.

The Golden Retriever was formally recognized by the English Kennel Club in 1913 as a "Yellow or Golden Retriever" with the "Yellow" dropped in 1920. Soon afterward, a group of British

In England around 1930, Mrs. Charlesworth with Noranby Sandy and Noranby Balfour. Sandy was the first breed member to run in field trials in England. She earned a number of certificates of merit.

retriever enthusiasts formed the Golden Retriever Club of England.

The first Golden left England in 1894, a lovely lass named Lady, owned by the Honorable Archie Marjoriebanks, Lord Tweedmouth's youngest son. Lady was taken to Canada, and later to Archie's ranch in Texas, becoming the first Golden to travel overseas. More Goldens reached Canada and the United States around 1900, most brought over by British Army officers and businessmen who often combined busi-

Ch. Gold-Rush Jersey Bounce at the JKC Tokyo Kita Club Rengo all-breed show.

Quartermoon Golden Randy with his first snow-covered wing. Breeder, Bobbie Christensen.

ness trips with the pleasures of hunting.

The American Kennel Club first recognized the Golden Retriever in 1925 with the registration of Lombardale Blondin, owned by Robert Appleton. Two years later the Canadian Kennel Club followed suit.

In 1930 the famous Speedwell Pluto of Rockhaven became the first American Golden Retriever bench champion. He was a splendid animal who was hunted hard and retrieved by the hour off the 20- and 30-foot cliffs into the icy waters of

Vancouver Bay. Pluto was big, powerful, handsome and courageous, and fortunately he reproduced himself in his offspring. He was one of the first dogs to enter the Golden Retriever Hall of Fame as an Outstanding Sire. (The Hall of Fame was established by the Golden Retriever Club of America to recognize and honor those dogs who produced champions or other accomplished dogs in their direct offspring.)

In the late 1930s, Paul Blakewell III of St. Louis gained prominence with his famous Golden Retriever Rip. Rip earned his Field Championship in 1939 and won the

A Golden Retriever must have correct structure to perform well in the field.

coveted *Field and Stream* trophy as the Outstanding Retriever in America in 1939, and again in 1940.

It is important to note that those Goldens who claimed bench awards during those early years were all hunting dogs who were hunted hard and often during their careers in the conformation ring.

In 1938 the Golden Retriever Club of America was formed to direct the destiny of the breed in the United States. As Goldens gained popularity in the U.S., more people brought them into the cities and suburbs. As a result of urban sprawl, game became less available in those areas, and dog fanciers

Goldens are natural athletes, therefore natural Frisbee®* dogs. Honor's Cogan in the Rockies UDTX, WC, TDI with Honor's Who's On First TDX, WC, TDI owned by Ron Buksaitis. *The trademark Frisbee is used under license from Mattel, Inc., California, USA.

Today they spread from Maine to Florida, and across the Midwest to California and Oregon. Because of their double coat, they can endure both heat and cold, are excellent swimmers and are especially effective in the lakes and rivers of the Midwest where game abounds.

The modern Golden Retriever has evolved into the most accomplished of all the retriever breeds. Goldens participate in and excel at more activities than any other breed of dog...conformation, obedience, field trials, hunting and hunting tests, tracking, agility, flyball and yes, even Frisbee®.

It's no surprise then

redirected their interest to Goldens as bench and obedience competitors and family companion dogs.

The Golden Retriever has nosed its way into every facet of the human-canine assistant connection. Support Dog Clancy obviously adores his owner Rosie Benecke.

Flint is a favorite camera subject for his owner, attorney/photographer Joe Spignola.

intuitive therapy dogs in hospitals and nursing homes, drug and arson detection dogs and search-and-rescue dogs, more roles than any of their canine brothers and sisters.

that the Golden has also nosed its way into every facet of the human-canine assistant connection. They serve as devoted guide dogs for the blind and hearing impaired, expert assistance dogs for the physically disabled and handicapped, gentle and

Yet despite their grand accomplishments, and with characteristic devotion and humility, they're still happiest sharing a bowl of popcorn or snuggled up beside your easy chair. The "Golden" Retriever could not be more aptly named.

Standard for the Golden Retriever

All breeds of dogs registered with the national kennel club are guided by a "standard," or formal description, which dictates the characteristics of a particular breed of dog and serves to direct the future of that breed. The standard for Golden Retrievers is brief and concise and follows in its entirety.

To produce good offspring, one must begin with sound adults that conform to the standard as closely as possible. This is puppy "Ruby" bred by the author and owned by Mike Sullivan.

Ch. Sunshine Hill's Nat'l Cowboy, bred by James and Cindy Lichtenberger, is owned by Elaine Fraze.

When choosing a puppy, remember that it has a lot of growing up to do. Be patient with puppy...she'll be a big girl far too soon. Meet the very fetching Karl's Lady Taffy.

General Appearance—A symmetrical, powerful, active dog, sound and well put together, not clumsy nor long in the leg, displaying a kindly expression and possessing a personality that is eager, alert and self-confident. Primarily a hunting dog, he should be shown in hard working condition. Overall appearance, balance, gait and purpose to be given more emphasis than any of his component parts.

Faults: Any departure from the described ideal shall be considered faulty to the degree to which it interferes with the breed's purpose or is contrary to breed character.

The Golden Retriever should possess a personality that is eager, alert and self confident. Apache, training buddy and best friend of owner Phil Bauer.

Size, Proportion, Substance—Males 23–24 inches in height at withers; females $21 \frac{1}{2}$ – $22 \frac{1}{2}$ inches. Dogs up to one inch above or below standard should be proportionately penalized. Deviation in height of more than one inch from the standard shall *disqualify.*

Length from breastbone to point of buttocks slightly greater than height at withers in ratio of 12:11. Weight for dogs 65-75 pounds; bitches 55-65 pounds.

Head—Broad in **skull,** slightly arched laterally and longitudinally without prominence of frontal bones (forehead) or occipital bones. **Stop** well defined but not abrupt. **Foreface** deep and wide, nearly as long

"Awesome," owned by Artie Awe, tries to smile like a duck.

as skull. **Muzzle** straight in profile, blending smoothly and strongly into skull; when viewed in profile or from above, slightly deeper and wider at stop than at tip. No heaviness in flews. Removal of whiskers is permitted but not preferred.

Eyes friendly and intelligent in expression, medium large with dark, close fitting rims, set well apart and reasonably deep in sockets. Color preferably dark brown; medium brown acceptable. Slant eyes and narrow, triangular eyes detract from correct expression and are to be faulted. No white or haw visible when looking straight ahead. Dogs showing evidence of functional abnormality of eyelids or eyelashes (such as, but not limited to, trichiasis, entropion, ectropion, or distichiasis) are to be excused from the ring.

Ears rather short with front edge attached well behind and just above the eye and falling close to the cheek. When pulled forward tip of ear should just cover the eye. Low, houndlike ear set to be faulted.

Nose black or brownish black, though fading to a lighter shade in cold weather not serious. Pink nose or one seriously lacking in pigmentation to be faulted.

Teeth scissors bite, in which the outer side of the lower incisors touches the inner side of the upper incisors. Undershot or overshot bite is a ***disqualification.*** Misalignment of teeth (irregular placement of incisors) or a level bite (incisors meet each other edge to edge) is undesirable, but not to be confused with undershot or overshot. Full dentition. Obvious gaps are serious faults.

Neck, Topline, Body—*Neck* medium long, merging gradually into well laid back shoulders, giving sturdy, muscular appearance. Untrimmed natural ruff. No throatiness.

Backline strong and

Golden puppy Fiddler, owned by Craig and Debbie Stocks, will eventually grow into his ears and feet!

level from withers to slightly sloping croup, whether standing or moving. Sloping backline, roach or sway back, flat or steep croup to be faulted. **Body** well balanced, short coupled, deep through the chest. **Chest** between forelegs at least as wide as a man's closed hand including thumb, with well developed forechest. Brisket extends to elbow. Ribs long and well sprung but not barrel shaped, extending well towards hindquarters. **Loin** short, muscular, wide and deep, with very little tuck-up. Slabsidedness, narrow chest, lack of depth in

Sextons Kona Gold owned by Karen and Jim Taylor. Karen lives in Taylor Michigan and is one of the most celebrated dog photographers in the US. Many of her photos grace this book.

brisket, excessive tuck-up to be faulted.

Tail well set on, thick and muscular at the base, following the natural line of the croup. Tail bones extend to, but not below, the point of hock. Carried with merry action, level or with some moderate upward curve; never curled over back nor between legs.

Forequarters— Muscular, well coordinated with hindquarters and capable of free movement. ***Shoulder blades*** long and well laid back with upper tips fairly close together at withers. ***Upper arms*** appear about the same length as the blades, setting the elbows back beneath the upper tip of

Sunclad Streaker's Jupiter UD retrieves the catch of the day for owner Barbara Branstad.

the blades, close to the ribs without looseness. ***Legs***, viewed from the front, straight with good bone, but not to the point of coarseness. ***Pasterns*** short and strong, sloping slightly with no suggestion of weakness. Dewclaws on forelegs may be removed, but are normally left on.

Feet medium size, round, compact and well-knuckled, with thick pads. Excess hair may be trimmed to show natural size and contour. Splayed or hare feet to be faulted.

Hindquarters— Broad and strongly muscled. Profile of croup slopes slightly; the pelvic bone slopes at a slightly greater angle (approximately 30 degrees from horizontal). In a natural stance, the femur joins the pelvis at approximately a 90 degree angle; **stifles** well bent; **hocks** well let

Legend's Bella Donna at seven weeks owned by Lisa Loew and Vicki Rathubun.

The Golden's water-repellent coat should be a rich lustrous golden color of various shades.

down with short, strong *rear pasterns.* **Feet** as in front. **Legs** straight when viewed from the rear. Cow hocks, spread hocks, and sickle hocks to be faulted.

Coat—Dense and water-repellent with good undercoat. Outer coat firm and resilient, neither coarse nor silky, lying close to the body; may be straight or wavy. Untrimmed natural ruff; moderate feathering on back of forelegs and on under-body; heavier feathering on front of neck, back of thighs

"Kirby," at six months enjoying the snow. Owned by Debbie Stremke.

and underside of tail. Coat on head, paws, and front of legs is short and even. Excessive length, open coats, and limp, soft coats are very undesirable. Feet may be trimmed and stray hairs neatened, but the natural appearance of coat should not be altered by cutting or clipping.

Color—Rich, lustrous golden of various shades. Feathering may be lighter than rest of coat. With the exception of graying or whitening of face or body due to age, any white markings, other than a few hairs on the chest, should be penalized according to its extent. Allowable light shadings are not to be confused with white markings. Predominant body color which is extremely pale or extremely dark is undesirable. Some latitude should be given to the light puppy whose coloring shows promise of deepening with maturity. Any noticeable area of black or other off-color hair is a serious fault.

Gait—When trotting, gait is free, smooth, powerful and well coordinated, showing good reach. Viewed from any position, legs turn neither in nor out, nor do feet cross or interfere with each other. As speed increases, feet tend to converge toward a center line of balance. It is recommended that dogs be shown on a loose lead to reflect true gait.

Temperament— Friendly, reliable, and trustworthy. Quarrel-

This handsome fellow is "Augie" owned by Dan and Pat Cook.

someness or hostility towards other dogs or people in normal situations, or an unwarranted show of timidity or nervousness, is not in keeping with Golden Retriever character. Such action should be penalized according to their significance.

Disqualifications

1. *Deviation in height of more than one inch from standard either way.*

2. *Undershot or overshot bite.*

COMMENTS

Without an accepted guideline, purebred dogs could be bred without regard to color,

Tyler Keever plants a gentle kiss on his best friend Chaser.

The author's Golden dozen in their outdoor playpen.

structure, temperament or natural instinct. After several generations of undisciplined breeding, any breed of dog might no longer resemble or behave like the one it was originally intended to be.

With Goldens, sadly, a dimension of that occurs despite the above standard approved by the AKC Board of Directors in 1982. Today we often see Goldens weighing well over 100 pounds, many with structural defects that affect their health and longevity and render the animal useless for hunting, retrieving, or even active play within the family. We see Goldens with markings and colors far outside the acceptable range as described in the stan-

Proud momma "Misty" and her seven Golden gems. Owned by Carol Sprague. Ancestry affects offspring, and good breeding is essential to keep this breed "Golden" forever.

dard. Moreover, the "friendly, reliable, trustworthy" Golden temperament is also disappearing today, leaving in its wake many Goldens who are not only hostile and quarrelsome but often outright aggressive with other dogs and people.

If the Golden Retriever continues to be bred without guidelines or scruples or without adequate knowledge of how a dog's ancestry affects its offspring, this lovely and gentle animal eventually will be "Golden" no longer.

Is a Golden Retriever Right for You?

When adding a canine companion to your home or family, the selection process is three-fold: choose a breed, then a reliable source for your pup, and, finally, the puppy—in that order.

First ask yourself why you want a dog and what you're looking for in this canine friend. Dogs purchased on a whim or without enough serious reflection usually end up in animal shelters. Unfor-

You should be certain that a Golden Retriever will fit into your lifestyle before committing to a dog. This is Dande Lion Delight, "Casey," owned by Bonnie Rubin.

tunately people often spend more time re-searching and shopping for their automobile than they do their dog, even though the animal will live in their home (not the garage), will love them, and serve them many more years than their vehicle. If more people were well-in-formed when they puppy-shopped, there would be fewer abused and abandoned dogs on the street or euthanized in animal shelters.

Your new canine companion will depend entirely upon you for its physical and emotional needs. Zack and Ziggy keep a watchful eye on their feathered friend. Owner, Nancy Cutu-Melka.

Before getting a dog of any breed, you must be absolutely con-vinced the animal will improve the quality of your life, and be totally committed to do your utmost to contribute to the quality of the animal's life. Your canine companion will depend entirely upon you for its physical and emotional needs. (If you don't agree that dogs have emotional needs, you will be happier with a hamster or guinea pig for a pet.)

Before getting any breed of dog, you must be convinced that the animal will improve the quality of your life. Chelsea was the Gaines Dog Hero of the Year when she was wounded while saving owner Chris Dittmar from two robbers armed with handguns.

If you're considering a Golden Retriever, first ask yourself some important questions. Will this animal be a house pet, hunting dog, show dog, obedience or field trial competitor? A lap dog? Contrary to some popular images of the "typical" Golden, this is a high-energy sporting dog who will require a great deal of daily attention. Will your disposition and lifestyle be compatible with a lively animal who will demand a generous amount of your time and energy?

Do you expect your dog to be a home protector? The typical Golden's "Glad To Meet

You" attitude would not deter a home intruder, especially one familiar with the Golden's friendly reputation.

Size is an important consideration. That adorable Golden puppy will grow up...and up...and up, into a 50- to 75-pound adult. All that puppy energy will multiply as well! Goldens mature slowly and their inquisitive and spirited disposition persists well into adulthood.

Will dog hair on your suit or sofa drive you wild? The "fuzzy" charm of a Golden puppy will blossom into a thick fur coat that will require frequent brushing to keep it out of your soup and salad bowl...Goldens aren't particular about where they deposit their fur. They lose their heavy winter undercoat in spring and shed a little every day, all year long. Regular twice-weekly grooming will keep shedding to a minimum, but Golden owners eventually get used to dog hair on their clothes and furniture.

Don't forget pawprints...often through your garden and across your kitchen floor. Most Golden puppies and adults love to get wet and will happily splash about in every puddle they find. Play and potty time in muddy yards or rainy weather present extra problems for owners of wet-type dogs with big feet. If

Red Eagle Just Do It Nike CD, TD, JH, WC, owned by Sue Hawxhurst, pregnant with her first litter (of 12 puppies). Typical of a very "oral" Golden, Nike carries not one, but two shoes at a time!

you covet spotless floors or object to towel-drying a hairy wet dog, think twice about a Golden Retriever.

If after all those considerations you're still thinking of adding

Pretty puppy Penny peeks over her tip-proof food and water bowls. Owned and loved by the Johnson family.

a Golden Retriever to your family, it's a good idea also to examine your living situation. Do you live in a house, condominium or apartment? Will your household accommodate a large and active animal? Is there a fenced-in yard in which to air and exercise the dog? The average Golden is a large dog who requires lots of exercise and loves to run. Few Goldens adapt well to small, cramped living quarters nor will they thrive without long walks or other physical and mental stimulation.

Be realistic about your own physical, financial, and time limitations. If you live in an apartment, if you

The author's special friend, Chances R Mein Leibschen CDX, WC, TDI, CGC and feline pal, JD.

cannot commit to a daily routine that will satisfy a Golden's emotional and physical needs, if you cannot afford the time or cost of feeding, grooming, vetting and properly caring for a Golden Retriever, please reconsider your breed of choice. Perhaps a smaller, less active dog would better suit your situation and lifestyle. Perhaps an older dog who is already housebroken and has had some basic obedience training would be easier to handle. Adult and rescue Goldens often are happy alternatives for people ill-equipped for puppy life.

Planning the Puppy Search

When you add a dog to your family or household, you begin a relationship that will span the next 10 to 15 years, so you can't learn enough about your chosen breed. A thorough "Golden education" will assure you of a quality puppy and adult who possesses the gentle temperament that has raised the breed to its current level of popularity.

Breed literature is a basic and important aspect of breed re-

Try to visit several breeders and view the litter as many times as you can before you select a puppy and bring it home. These puppies are enjoying a ride in kiddie cars.

Cuddling and gentle handling are an important part of puppy socialization with children and people.

search. The Golden Retriever Club of America publishes two booklets to educate prospective Golden owners, and anyone considering a Golden should read both. *Acquiring a Golden Retriever* and *An Introduction to the Golden Retriever* are available through the GRCA secretary. Write to GRCA Secretary c/o Golden Retriever columnist, AKC, 51 Madison Ave., New York, NY 10010. Several good books on the Golden also are available in pet shops and book stores.

Talk to veterinarians, people who own Goldens and the breeders who bred those dogs. Ask about good and bad characteristics: no breed is perfect or flawless. Be sure to find Golden breeders who will be honest enough to tell you about the disadvantages and problems that come with owning a Golden Retriever. Learn about the nega-

An all-time puppy favorite...bathroom paper! Kirby is playing "grab-it-and-run." Solution...keep the bathroom door closed! Owner, Debbie Stremke.

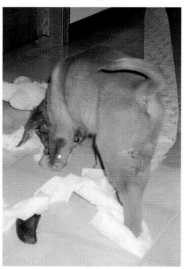

tive side now so you won't be surprised later on.

Most importantly, before you purchase a Golden Retriever, consider your long-term goals for this special pup. If you expect to hunt with your Golden, plan a career in the show or obedience ring, or hope to train it for hunting tests or field trials, you must find a breeder who raises Goldens for that purpose. Whatever your goals for your pup, working dog or full-time family companion, your Golden must be emotionally stable and physically sound.

It might be wise to prepare a "puppy list" before beginning your puppy search.

This lovely pup known as "Cricket" was bred by Janet Edmonds.

1. Establish your goals for this puppy. Hunter? Show ring star? Obedience competitor? Children's companion? What are you ABLE to do vs. what do you HOPE to do with your Golden?

2. Research breeders and pedigrees. Learn how to read a pedigree. What is line breeding, inbreeding, outcrossing? What do titles or letters mean before and after a dog's name?

3. Make a list of questions to ask breeders and Golden owners about health, temperament, working ability, trainability. Be specific with your questions. Don't just ask about cataracts or good hips; ask about CERF and OFA (Ca-

Playing with littermates is a critical part of canine socialization. Never take a pup home too young—seven to nine weeks is ideal. These two Cattail Golden pups were bred by Eileen Bohn.

nine Eye Registry Foundation and Orthopedic Foundation for Animals, the two screening agents for canine eyes and hips). A wise puppy shopper is prepared BEFORE the search begins!

4. Visit dog shows, obedience trials, hunting tests. Watch the dogs in action...what do you like about certain Golden Retrievers? Ask the owners and handlers about their dogs. Most Golden owners love to talk about the breed, especially their own dogs, and will gladly answer questions and offer information. Find out who bred the dogs you like and how you can contact those breeders. Pick up a program or catalog of

the dogs entered to find the names and addresses of their owners.

5. Armed with your battery of questions, pursue several breeders and owners to inquire about their dogs. This may involve many letters and phone calls, but your future pup is worth the time and effort.

Ask about health clearances and genetic problems such as hip dysplasia, elbow dis-

Dog shows and obedience trials are great places to talk to Golden breeders and learn about the breed. OTCh. DD's Tagalong Thumper TD, JH, WC, Can. CDX (OS), owned by DeeDee Anderson, takes a high jump to celebrate his High-in-Trial award.

Your puppy's socialization skills will begin to develop while it is still with the breeder. An empty cardboard box proves to be a puppy favorite.

ease, epilepsy, allergies and skin problems. Inquire about temperament, energy level and willingness to please, as well as the physical properties of the dog, such as head, bite, coat and eye color, topline and gait. Ask how and where the pups are raised. In the house? (They better be.) Socialized with the family? (Absolutely!) Will the dewclaws be removed? (They should be.)

Don't hesitate to travel to find a quality breeder. But if you're too far away, ask the breeder to send a video of his or her dogs at home and in the field.

Ask any and all questions you may have before you bring your new pup home. Goldenbear puppy bred by Cindy Lichtenberger.

BREEDERS

The Golden you plan to raise with your children, hunt with, or take into the show or obedience ring must be physically sound and emotionally stable. The best source for such an animal is the "serious hobby breeder," an experienced breeder who not only is knowledgeable about the breed and attempts to produce the best quality pups possible but also takes full responsibility for every puppy produced.

Serious hobby breeders raise puppies not for profit, but because they love their chosen breed. They take special care to place their pups in the best homes possible. Good breeders always interview the prospective puppy family to make sure they will provide a proper and loving home for their pup. Because he or she is concerned about the long-term health and happiness of their little ones, the breeder will want to know all about YOU. Some

This is a puppy No-No! Never play tug-of-war with your pup. It encourages aggression and will threaten your position as top dog.

Sweet talk and encouragement are an important part of training a young Golden.

ence or hunting tests. That association with other breeders and sportsmen enhances the credibility of a reputable breeder and expands his/her knowledge of the breed and breed characteristics. Most Golden breeders love their dogs and puppies, but just loving your dog like crazy doesn't qualify an individual to breed dogs intelligently or properly raise their pups.

interviews may even resemble the Spanish Inquisition. Be patient...that breeder really cares.

Expect the breeder to be involved in some aspect of the dog fancy with his/her dog(s), perhaps showing in conformation or obedi-

Reputable breeders should be able to provide references from other breeders and puppy buyers as well as veterinarians who have cared for his/her dogs. The breeder should offer a purchase contract and provide a written guarantee on the health of the puppies. A typical take-home package for new puppy families should include the AKC blue registration slip (or a written guarantee that the blue slip is forthcoming from AKC), a three-to-five generation pedigree of the sire and dam (the registration and pedigree are NOT the same), copies of both parents' health clearances, puppy's health record of shots and wormings, and a full set of instructions on how to care for this

Chances R Chasin' Rainbows with one-week-old litter of pups owned by David and Kim Keever. Breeders often color-code pups with rick-rack ribbon to monitor each pup's individual development more closely.

special puppy. The breeder should also be willing, indeed anxious, to check up on puppy's progress and be available if you have questions or problems with the pup.

Expect to pay a dear price for a properly-bred Golden puppy with a sound pedigree, more for pups with show and field potential. The "discount" Golden puppy is not a bargain—it's a potential disaster that has little chance of growing into a healthy, stable adult and could ultimately cost you a fortune in dollars and heartache.

In order to guarantee healthy Golden puppies, responsible breeders test the sire and dam for hereditary disease common to Golden Retrievers. They should provide OFA (Orthopedic Foundation for Animals) records that certify the parents have been x-rayed and cleared for hip dysplasia, CERF (Canine Eye Registry Foundation) or ophthalmologist reports of eye examinations within the past year, and proof that both dogs have been tested for freedom from von Willebrand's disease and hereditary heart disease.

Statements like "We don't need an x-ray, she has great hips; you should see her clear our five-foot fence" or "We've never had a problem with our puppies in the past" are

Before breeding a litter of pups, a responsible breeder will test the sire and dam for hereditary diseases that the Golden is more prone to than other breeds.

Puppies should be exposed to humans at an early age so they will not grow up fearful and people-shy and unable to bond with their human family.

not be affected by these serious health problems. Heed the warnings of a California family who didn't know about hereditary defects and bought their puppy from a breeder who didn't OFA certify. "Our dog has degenerative arthritis resulting from hip dysplasia. He's been on steroid treatments for three and one-half years and now he's having problems caused by the steroids. It's tragic and so unfair."

proof only of careless breeding practices, and you should avoid them at all costs. Proper health clearance certificates on the sire and dam help to ensure their offspring will

WHERE TO FIND A BREEDER

In addition to dog shows and obedience trials and hunt tests, local veterinarians are an excellent resource; ask not one, but several, for the names of members of the area Golden Retriever club. Those people can refer you to litters bred by club members. There are many reliable breeders outside the family of Golden Retriever clubs, but there is greater risk and inconvenience in locating them and verifying their credibility. Remember, when you buy a puppy, you also buy the breeder's expertise and understanding of the breed.

If there are no Golden Retriever clubs in your vicinity, you can write to the American Kennel Club or The Kennel Club for the name and address of the current secretary of the national Golden Retriever club to obtain information on the club nearest you. In Canada, write the Canadian Kennel Club, 2150 Bloor St. West, Toronto, Ontario M6S 4V7.

You can obtain information about the Golden Retriever club nearest you by writing to the national kennel club. This is AFC KC's Chip Off The Ole Block MH at five months, proudly owned by Roger Fuller.

Once you locate a reliable breeder, you may have to wait a while for the right litter. Remember, the right pup is worth the wait!

Upon finding a breeder you feel you can trust, you may have to wait a while for the right litter. Be patient! A wise choice now will reward you with a healthy, stable pup and a lifetime of love your new Golden will happily share with you.

The Right Puppy for You

All purebred puppies should come with AKC registration papers—proof that the sire and dam are the parents of the pup. An AKC registration, however, does NOT

This is Chances R Gingersnap at ten weeks, owned by Yvonne Pertle.

guarantee quality, health or stability.

Haven't we all heard, "It's a good pup; it has papers, is AKC registered, etc."? That is, sadly, the biggest myth in the pet world of purebred dogs. The American Kennel Club is merely a registry of dog breeds, and "papers" are simply AKC's confirmation that a puppy's parents are of the same breed. It does not in any way guarantee that puppy or its parents are in good health, have good temperaments or are not affected by any hereditary disease. Further, every month the AKC Board of Directors fines and suspends many individuals for falsifying paperwork and keeping improper records (of who sired whom...) in their dog breeding businesses. That's just one warning flag to alert an unsuspecting puppy-buying public.

The AKC registration also is not the dog's pedigree, which is the pup's family tree, a three- to five-generation list of its ancestors. The ancestors' names will also bear any title designations that indicate a championship or degree of merit they have earned in areas of canine competition. Occasionally "championship lines" in a pedigree are promoted by an inexperienced or disreputable breeder,

Puppies need a variety of toys for stimulation and to satisfy their need to chew. The safest chew toys for puppies are made by Nylabone® and are available in pet shops.

when in fact the only champion in the dog's heritage may have been one lone Ch. (Show Champion) four generations back. A smart puppy shopper should become familiar with purebred terminology.

The first rule of puppy selection is "Take your time." Most Golden puppies can steal your heart with one sweet puppy kiss, but you must resist the irresistible to find a healthy and problem-free Golden.

When you visit a litter, scrutinize the

Your Golden puppy will be curious about everything it comes into contact with. Puppy "China" meets Dakota owned by Kevin Kilgore.

Summer puppies can receive an early introduction to water in a child's wading pool with a doorway cut in the side.

puppies and their environment carefully for cleanliness and possible signs of poor health or sickness. A healthy puppy should have bright, clear eyes and a clean, thick coat. Beware of a runny or crusted discharge from the eyes, ears or nose. Puppies should be well proportioned and feel solid and muscular, without a pot-bellied appearance. They should be bright-eyed, energetic and alert. Their stools should be firm and well formed without any sign of blood. The puppy environment should be clean and well tended.

Golden puppies can range in color from varying shades of pale blond to dark buff or tan. Coat color will darken with age. The puppy's ears are a

Kelsey graciously allows baby brother Jack to rest piggyback on "her" couch.

good adult coat barometer; darker ears indicate the puppy will be a darker gold or red when he grows up. White markings are not acceptable in the show ring, but don't affect a dog's role as a hunting partner or family companion.

Visit with the dam and sire if at all possible, and spend time observing the parents with their pups. Notice how the pups react to their surroundings, especially their response to people, and watch how they interact with their littermates. The puppies should be active, robust and bouncy. Some may be more outgoing than others, but even a quiet little guy who is well-socialized should not shrink at a friendly voice or outstretched hand.

During your visit some puppies may be tired or freshly awakened from a nap, so the dominant pup may be sleepy and unresponsive, while the bashful boy could be wide awake and charging at his littermates. Therefore it's wise to visit a litter more than

Some puppies may be tired or freshly awakened from a nap when you come to visit, so it's best to visit a litter more than once, if possible. Raindancer's Brilliant Flare at nine weeks. Owner, Sally Jenkins.

Exploring a cardboard box tunnel is part of a pup's early introduction to new learning adventures.

interest in people or its surroundings. Roll a ball or toy to test for self-assurance and a strong chase instinct. Golden puppies are very "oral" and will generally retrieve and carry any object that will fit in their mouth.

Also observe the personality of the dam, and sire if he is available. Behavior is inherited, and if the parent(s) are aggressive or very shy, the pups likely will inherit those characteristics.

once before making your puppy selection.

Evaluate several puppies individually, apart from their littermates. Clap your hands and move away to see if a puppy will follow you. Avoid a puppy who shows no desire to play or lacks

Pick a pup whose personality will most suit your goals and lifestyle. The puppy who tears about at full-speed, jumps at your face and nips your fingertips may be too much for a quiet, passive individual. A quiet littermate who licks your hand and is less wiggly and more relaxed will be more apt to accept its new human as its pack leader and will be easier to train.

The breeder can help you select a puppy best suited to your needs and goals. Remember, a good breeder has spent most of the past seven or eight weeks feeding, cuddling and cleaning up after the entire litter and knows the subtle differences in each pup's personality.

If you plan to show your Golden in conformation, a breeder who raises Goldens for that purpose can help you

At five weeks this litter of 12 pups has outgrown one flying saucer feeding pan and now requires two.

Four-month-old pup in puppy class. Author Nona Kilgore Bauer coaxes puppy to walk beside her.

evaluate a puppy's potential for the show ring. Show prospects are "stacked" and scrutinized at an early age to examine the physical properties of the developing puppy. The breeder should be happy to explain and demonstrate the process.

If your dream puppy will be a hunting companion, hunt test or field trial hopeful, you need a breeder who raises field Goldens and tests the pups for birdiness and a strong desire to retrieve. These pups are introduced to birds at five or six weeks of age and evaluated for eagerness and intensity when playing and retrieving. Look for a pup who wags its tail like crazy at the very sight or scent of birds. Field dogs who display a willingness to please also do well in the obedience ring.

The breeder's recommendations combined with your own educated observations are your best tools for selecting a puppy who will match your personality and lifestyle.

Preparing Puppy's Home

PUPPY-PROOFING

To provide a safe and carefree homecoming for your new Golden, you must puppy-proof your house beforehand to avoid any accidents or surprises that could be dangerous and even fatal for the pup.

1. Fasten electrical cords to baseboards or move them out of puppy's reach. Pups who chew on electrical cords can be seriously

Provide a safe homecoming for your new pup. Puppy-proof your house before you bring him home. Karl's Lady Taffy fetches firewood for owner Karl Baumwell.

burned from electric shock and may even die.

2. Keep medication bottles, cleaning agents and similar materials out of open areas where puppy can reach them. A determined puppy can chew the cap off even a heavy bottle of detergent.

3. Never use pesticides, roach, rodent or other poisons in any areas accessible to the puppy. Don't take anything for granted...puppies get into impossible-to-reach places.

4. Always keep the lid down on the toilet to eliminate the temp-

Golden puppies are eternally curious and must investigate everything.

Don't leave cans of food or garbage where they may be accessible to your Golden. This young dog learned to pry the lid off her food can.

tation for puppy to drink from the bowl. Avoid the use of bowl cleaners in case puppy gets into the water somehow.

5. Keep the trash secured where puppy can't dig after chicken bones and other tempting garbage that could choke or harm him.

6. Anti-freeze is extremely toxic to animals and even a few drops can kill an adult Golden. Dogs are

Christmas can be a potentially dangerous time for your Golden pup with the shiny objects, plants and holiday bustle. This is Legend's Christmas Dream, "Winston," owned by Mary Donahey.

attracted to its sweet taste, so clean up all spills in the garage and on the driveway immediately. Keep containers locked or well secured.

7. Check your house and yard for plants that might be toxic to dogs. Rhododendron, Japanese Yew, Poinsettia, Lily of the Valley and many house plants number among more than two dozen indoor and outdoor plants that can cause illness or death if eaten. A complete list is available at your local library. Your

Many outdoor plants and shrubs are potentially dangerous to your dog. Investigate the foliage around your home carefully for your pet's safety.

Proper socialization forms the foundation of the human-Golden relationship.

veterinarian may also have detailed information.

8. Weed killers and other herbicides can be toxic to animals and children. Some have residual effects for up to four weeks, and many are suspected of causing cancer in the long-term. Many dog owners prefer to live with a few weeds in order to promote a longer life for their pet.

9. Remove cigarettes and cigarette butts from ashtrays. Ingested cigarettes can lead to nicotine poisoning.

10. At Christmas, keep all decorations out of puppy's reach. Pups can dispose of a dangling glass ornament or fiberglass angel in the blink of an eye. Chocolate is also

Be sure that everyone in the home knows the correct way to hold the puppy. Children should always be supervised by adults when playing with the new Golden Retriever.

highly toxic to dogs as it contains a chemical called theobromine they are unable to process. Hide those chocolate Santas and other chocolate treats from your puppy and adult dogs. You don't need an emergency trip to the vet on a holiday eve.

Lawn fertilizers and flea control products can be dangerous to puppies. Be sure to read the ingredients carefully and check with your veterinarian before you allow the pup to play in the yard after it's been treated.

11. Be extremely careful when using flea-control products on or around puppies. Many are toxic to puppies and young dogs, and combining certain incompatible flea products can cause a toxic, even fatal reaction in dogs of any age. Always consult your vet for safe anti-flea strategy and use only as directed.

12. Puppy-proof your children. One sad statistic tells us that many pets are given up because of problems between the animal and the child or children. Child psychologists now

realize that very young children do NOT have a natural affinity for animals, rather they are unfeeling because they do not fully understand and often are cruel in their attitudes toward them.

Teach your children...and their friends...that this puppy is a living creature who is a friend and companion, not a toy to sit on or drag about. Show them how to be gentle and properly handle the pup. Never leave young children alone with your puppy; a playful

Puppies are very susceptible to illness and disease before they receive their permanent shots. Your veterinarian will provide a complete vaccination schedule.

puppy nip is painful and can easily break the skin, leaving the child fearful and resentful of the puppy. Conversely, even innocent child's play can result in serious injury to a pup.

Teach older children the correct way to hold a puppy, with a firm grip under the chest and stomach so the puppy can't wiggle and fall. Never allow them to carry puppy around; he can easily injure himself in even a short fall.

Teach all the children to respect puppy's needs and privacy. They must allow him time and space for naps and meals and puppy play. Puppies need "down time" just like children do.

Be sure you've stocked up on puppy supplies before you bring the little one home. The following

Children should respect puppy's needs, as well as those of the adult dog. Your Golden will respond better to your child if it is treated with love and respect. This is five-month-old Sadie kissing her four-year-old girlfriend, Ashley Marsala.

Stock up on puppy supplies before you bring your new Golden home. Be sure to select a water bowl that is non-tippable.

A soft bed and a Gumabone® chew toy will comfort your new Golden pup when you first bring him home.

items will provide a basic "puppy starter kit." Your vet may recommend additional items as well.

Food Bowls—You'll need separate bowls for food and water; two-quart, non-tippable stainless steel pans are preferred, as both plastic and aluminum can be chewed up and swallowed.

Collar—Puppies should get used to wearing a collar for identification and training purposes. A lightweight nylon web collar with a metal or plastic quick-release buckle is good for puppies and young dogs, although the plastic buckles are not sturdy enough for the adult Golden. Rolled leather collars are made specifically for long-haired breeds and won't damage the fur on your dog's neck, but some leather dyes may stain the coat. Puppies and adults should always wear an identification tag, plus a rabies tag in those places where that is required. Never put the dog's name on its collar, as that would enable a stranger or thief to call the dog and possibly claim it. Choke chain collars are for training purposes after the pup is five or six months old and must be worn ONLY during training sessions. Countless dogs have been hanged or choked to death when their choke collars snagged on a fence post, crate wire or other protrusion.

To measure your dog's neck for the correct size collar, use a flexible measuring tape around the circumference of the dog's neck. Add two inches to that

It is important to get your Golden pup used to wearing a collar for identification and training purposes. Puppies grow quickly—be sure to check the collar frequently.

measurement to determine the proper collar size. Most nylon web collars with quick-release buckles come in three sizes that will adjust and expand about two inches as the dog grows and should fit a puppy for the first three months. Check the collar often during the first six- month rapid-growth period; some puppies seem to grow out of their collars overnight.

Leash—A lightweight leash made of nylon web material, four-to six-foot length, makes a good puppy-starter lead. A six-foot leather leash is the standard lead for walking your adult dog and for obe-

A lightweight nylon web leash makes a good puppy-starter lead.

dience training classes (wait until puppy is through teething!). A flexi-lead—an 8-to 16-foot retractable leash that reels in automatically—and a 20- to 30-foot lightweight nylon rope or line are also handy for exercising your puppy, especially in unfenced areas or when traveling.

Chew Toys—Puppies are tiny chewing machines. Just like toddlers, they need toys to keep them happily occupied and chew objects to satisfy their natural chewing instincts. Nylabones® and Gumabones® come in several shapes and sizes appropriate for every age and breed and are virtually indestructible. Discard and replace them when the

Gumabones® are made of non-toxic, durable polyurethane and satisfy the puppy's chewing needs.

knobby ends become very rough and worn away. Puppies also enjoy nylon rope toys like Nylafloss®.

Large beef knuckle bones or large sterilized natural bones

The Nylafloss® by Nylabone® is not only a chew toy but a dental floss as well. It helps in the removal of your puppy's baby teeth by gently pulling on them as the nylon slips through. Never buy cotton rope devices—nylon only!

available in pet stores and pet supply catalogs are also favorite chew objects. They do not readily splinter, and most dogs simply gnaw them down over a period of time. Never give a puppy or adult dog steak, chicken or pork bones. They splinter easily and can cause choking and often internal bleeding when swallowed.

Brush and Comb—A slicker brush is the best tool for routine brushing sessions with your Golden. A steel comb with wide and narrow-spaced teeth is more efficient when grooming during heavy shedding season. Mat rakes, shedding combs and several other optional tools also work well on a thick Golden coat; check with your breeder or a local dog groomer for tips on proper grooming aids.

Shampoo—Use a mild shampoo with conditioners to bathe your Golden puppy and adult. Don't bathe your dog routinely or too frequently simply for the sake of bathing, rather only when he's gotten into something unpleasant, has an offensive body odor, or when his coat gets soiled or lacks luster. Too many baths will strip the natural oils from his coat. Twice-weekly brushing will clean the dust and debris from the coat and eliminate the need for frequent bathing.

Ear Cleansing Solution—Long-eared breeds like Goldens frequently collect dirt and waxy matter in their ears. Clean the inside of the ear flap

Accustom your Golden puppy to grooming at an early age and he'll learn to enjoy it as he grows up. Adult Goldens have more than enough coat to brush!

and external grooves in the outer ear regularly, and cleanse the ear canal as directed by your veterinarian whenever you find an accumulation of wax. Untended or neglected ears can lead to ear infections and a trip to the veterinarian.

First Aid Kit— Assemble a canine first aid kit before your puppy arrives so you always have emergency supplies... "just in case." Keep it separate from your family's first aid supplies and in a handy place where it won't get mixed up or used up with household items. Basic supplies include a canine first aid instruction book, rectal thermometer, syrup of ipecac to induce vomit-

ing, an anti-diarrheal safe for dogs, ear cleansing solution, gauze pads and vet wrap (a stick-to-itself gauze bandage wrap), cotton balls and swabs, hydrogen peroxide and petroleum jelly, tweezers, eye dropper and a small syringe without the needle for giving liquid medications. Be sure you read your first aid book *before* you need to use it so you'll be prepared for the unexpected.

Crate—The most important piece of equipment in your new puppy's home is his crate. A dog crate is a collapsible wire kennel or fiberglass airline shipping kennel, both available at most pet shops and in

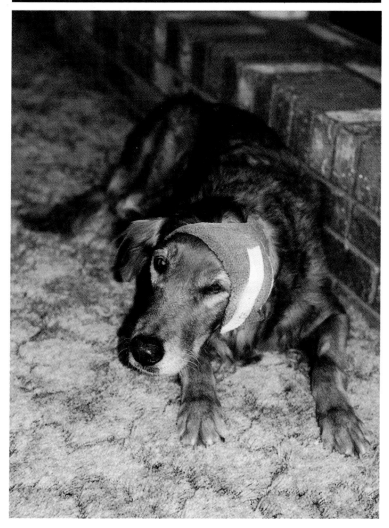

Have a canine first aid kit prepared before you need it. Leibschen tolerates a pressure bandage after surgery to remove a tumor.

Use a travel crate to ensure your Golden's safety while driving in the car or staying at motels.

pet supply catalogs. A crate is not cruel or unusual punishment, rather it's a secure area that will aid in housebreaking your pup, protect your furnishings when you're not home, provide a safe harbor to confine the dog when conditions require it, and afford safe travel accommodations for the dog while driving or staying at motels. A dog accustomed to crating also will accept occasional veterinary confinement without question and with less stress.

Purchase a crate that will accommodate an adult Golden; your puppy will grow into it. A 22-inch by 36-inch wire crate or "large retriever size" fiberglass airline crate will comfortably house the average full-grown Golden Retriever.

Welcome Home, Puppy!

Most canine behaviorists agree seven weeks or 49 days is the ideal age for a puppy to leave its littermates for a new home. At this age a pup is best able to begin the socialization process and form strong social bonds with humans. By seven weeks it is absolutely

Seven to nine weeks is the ideal age for a Golden puppy to leave its littermates for a new home.

Puppy "Irish" Huff at four-and-a
half-months old.

At eight weeks of age puppies enter what is known as the fear period, a critical time in puppy development when any frightening or traumatic experience could leave a lasting impression and result in long-term, fearful behavior. Sudden or very loud noises, rough handling or harsh discipline are just a few examples of incidents that could traumatize a pup.

It's important to provide a calm, nurturing environment during this tenuous eight to nine week period, while still allowing puppy to adjust to your normal household routine. Try to schedule trips to the veterinarian before or after the eighth week.

essential that puppies experience positive people contact. However, an older pup who has been well socialized by its breeder will be as well adjusted as the one who went to his new home at seven weeks.

(Some breeders choose to keep their puppies through this delicate stage and release them at nine or ten weeks of age.)

Plan to bring your puppy home at a time when you'll be able to spend the next several days quietly getting acquainted and introducing him to his new environment. Puppy's transition from his canine siblings to his new human pack should be as calm and stress-free as possible. A puppy shouldn't be subjected to a rousing welcome home from several neighborhood children

Bring your puppy home when you can spend the first several days together to help him adjust to his new environment.

Christmas trees and decorations are tantalizing temptations for curious puppies. Your tree should be off limits to your new pup.

and/or adults. Never bring a new pup home at Christmas or during a busy holiday period. An abundance of holiday cheer may be great fun for the family, but a pup newly separated from its mother and littermates will be terrified amid all the activity and noise in a strange environment.

A quiet, peaceful atmosphere will help relieve the anxiety of "leaving home." Rest assured that underneath that bouncing Golden fuzzball beats an anxious heart that's wondering, "Where's Mom?"

HOUSEBREAKING AND CRATE USE

Have your puppy's crate set up prior to his arrival and put it in a quiet "people" area of the house so he won't feel isolated from his new human pack. The importance of immediate crate use is critical. Statistics show most dogs are surrendered to animal shelters because of destructive behavior during the owner's absence. Correctly and humanely used, a crate reduces the potential for unacceptable behavior, keeping both the dog

Puppy Kirby asleep with her head under a chair, illustrating a pup's natural instinct to sleep in snug and enclosed places.

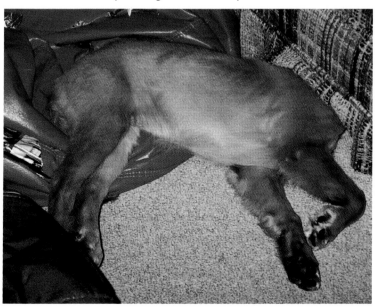

Your Golden Retriever pup is a natural den creature and will enjoy having a place such as this play box or a crate, where it can feel safe and secure.

as well as the house intact.

Like their wolf ancestors, dogs are natural den creatures. A crate satisfies that ancient tendency and affords the dog a place he understands and where he can feel safe and secure. Puppies are also inherently clean and will not soil their den unless they have no alternative, for instance, crated for too long a time. This natural instinct is your strongest housebreaking tool.

Crate use is not recommended if the puppy routinely must be left alone for extended periods of more than three hours at a time. If prolonged confinement is absolutely necessary, a secure outdoor kennel run is recommended. An exercise pen or collapsible wire enclosure also can be used to create a secure indoor area where puppy has a water supply and can eliminate when necessary. If you must be gone for long periods of time, you might recruit a relative or reliable friend to spend a mid-day hour with your pup to feed and play with him. For prospective Golden owners who cannot attend to a pup for extended day-time hours...you would be wise to consider a started pup or adult Golden. Fortunately most older dogs come "With love and ready to use!"

If you choose a wire kennel, you can cover it with an old sheet or blanket to emphasize the den-like environ-ment. If possible, move the crate into your bedroom at night to enhance the bonding process. If puppy whimpers during the night, just dangle your fingers inside the crate to remind him of your nearby presence. (Don't let him chew on them!) You'll also hear if he becomes restless so you can whisk him outside to eliminate.

Use a "puppy towel" to help transform your

Golden puppies love to sleep in pretzel positions.

Christmas is not a good time to bring a puppy into your household.

the towel will absorb the puppies' scent. Place the towel in your puppy's crate and the familiar smell of his brothers and sisters will lessen the trauma of leaving his litter-mates and make the crate seem more like home.

Encourage your puppy to enter his crate by tossing in a bit of puppy treat while pup is watching. Leave the food in the crate with the door open until he takes it, then praise him after he does so. You can also feed puppy his first meal or two in the crate with the door open to create a pleas-ant association. Leave a couple of safe chew toys in the crate so puppy can amuse

new puppy's crate into a more familiar envi-ronment. When you pick up your puppy from the breeder, bring a large bath towel and place it in with puppy's littermates for a while. Let them play with it, lie on it and drag it around if possible, so himself when he's crated and awake.

Most importantly, the crate must never be used as punishment; *never* scold the puppy and immediately put him in his crate. This is his safe and secure place and he should enter it with a positive attitude and associate it with only pleasant feelings.

Another cardinal rule of crate training...never call the puppy to you, then immediately put him in his crate. Puppies learn by association, and if their reward for coming to you is going into the crate, they will "come" with less and less enthusiasm and

A crate is the safest means of travel for your Golden. Both you and the dog will be more relaxed.

Starburst's Show Em Some Magic would have to be Houdini to escape this wire crate. Give puppy a couple of toys when he is in his crate. Owner, Karen Taylor.

soon resist coming whenever possible. For better results go to the pup and carry or walk him to his crate. Use a key word such as "Kennel" or "Crate" when crating the pup to teach him a crate entry command. Once he understands the "Crate" command, use that word consistently to direct puppy to his crate. "Jasper, crate," rather than "Jasper, come."

Leave the crate door open when puppy isn't in it so he can choose to enter the crate on his own when he wants to nap or "get away." Teach your children to not reach in and pull the puppy from the crate, rather to call him to come out willingly on his own.

Do not release the puppy from his crate while he's whining or pleading to get out. Wait until he settles down, even if only for a brief moment, then quietly allow him to come out. Always use a low-key approach when puppy goes in or out of the crate. Praise him softly upon entering his crate, but don't reward him with food, treats or praise when he's released. His reward is being once again with you.

Establish a crate routine for puppy, crating him at night, during naps, and whenever you're not able to watch him. If puppy falls asleep at your feet or under the table or sofa (further proof of that natural den instinct), just pick him up and place him in his crate to finish his nap. Now be sure to close the door so he'll have to let you

Keeping children out of crates seems more difficult than keeping pups in them.

Take your Golden pup outside immediately after he wakes up. Praise him lavishly when he has done what is expected of him.

know when he wakes up. Otherwise, guess what! He will probably hop quietly out of the open door, piddle nearby, then bounce over to say, "Hi!"

Always take puppy out to relieve himself each time he wakes up and/or leaves his

crate. With a young puppy, space very short periods between potty trips (use your oven timer for reminder); puppy control comes slowly, so patience and persistence are your most important housebreaking ingredients.

Puppies always need to eliminate when they first wake up in the morning, after naps and play time, within a very short time after eating, and before bed at night. Take pup outside as soon as he awakens and lavish him with praise as soon as he eliminates. You can select your own key word for his performance, such as "Hurry up" or "Get busy," then combine it with praise every time he goes. "Good boy, hurry up, good boy!" Pup will soon recognize his special word and get the message about those little trips outside.

You must accompany puppy on these outings, rain or snow, midnight or 3 a.m., so you can make sure he finishes his business. Even if you have a fenced yard, don't just let him trot outside by himself. Remember those key words...and key ingredients!

Always use the same exit or entrance to the house for puppy's

Wylie's not satisfied with one tennis ball; she wants two! Owners, Dan and Kathy Waldemar.

potty needs and the same place outdoors, so puppy will learn how to get to his appointed spot. Puppies will often urinate on a spot that they or another dog has previously anointed. (Why do you think fire hydrants are so popular?) You can

Puppies will often urinate on a spot that they or another dog previously anointed. Some pups may seem to sniff forever.

also use a bit of soiled newspaper or paper towel from an indoor accident to help show him the right spot in the yard.

Be observant and monitor your puppy's signals when he has to go out; sniffing the floor or circling and starting to squat. Once he understands where his outside area is, he may simply go to the door...period. Each dog develops his own message system...pacing, barking, pawing at the door, or just sitting next to the door, and if you're not there within seconds...puddle-time. It's up to you to be alert to these signs and make him as successful as possible when he "tells" you. Success will build on success.

Kelsey investigates a decoy during a puppy swimming lesson.

It's a good idea to confine your puppy to one or two small areas of the house at first. Baby gates are excellent for this. Then gradually introduce him to allowable areas of his new home, one room at a time, with sweet talk and encouragement so these strange places won't be so formidable. It's less stressful for a puppy to explore limited areas, and it will afford him more opportunity to learn the housebreaking routine. The

Most Golden puppies are not little angels with halos.

youngster who tags along while you make the beds upstairs will not remember how to navigate through several rooms and down a flight of stairs when he gets the urge to go.

Despite your best efforts, mistakes will still happen. If puppy has an accident indoors, forget it and try again later. NEVER discipline the puppy for an accident you discover after the fact; puppies cannot connect a correction with a past deed. Punishing him even seconds later will only cause fear and confusion. You must catch him IN the act. Then use a firm NO and carry him outside. NEVER strike him with your hand or a newspaper or rub the puppy's nose in his mistake. Such punishment will only create fearful behavior in the dog and can complicate and prolong the housebreaking process.

Finally remember that most puppy training revolves around repetition and word association. Use one- or two-syllable words and use the same words consistently for those behaviors you want to teach and

Your Golden's crate is the one place where he will feel secure, whether he is traveling or just relaxing at home. Never use the crate as a means of punishing your dog.

shape. Don't confuse the pup with unnecessary conversation. Simple, very basic communication is appropriate for a pup.

A popular cartoon titled "What We Say to Our Dogs," illustrates typical human-canine communication problems. The first cartoon shows the owner wagging his finger at the upended garbage can and scolding, "Okay, Ginger, I've had it! You stay out of the garbage! Understand, Ginger? Stay out or else!" The second cartoon panel is titled "What Dogs Hear." Same picture with the owners words, "Blah, blah, Ginger, blah, blah, blah, blah, Gin-

ger, blah blah!" All that extra conversation just amounts to nagging.

Your puppy will also respond to your body language and tone of voice. Later on...much later...your dog will hang on your every word, one of the many pleasures of a long-term partnership with a dog.

There are many books available today that specifically address the issues of puppy training and socialization. Technology has also blessed dog owners with several videos on educating and training a pup. Take advantage of them. You and your pup both will be smarter, and you'll be entertained along the way.

Golden's are natural water dogs and even pups as young as eight or nine weeks enjoy the wet stuff.

Puppy's Second-Best Friend: Your Veterinarian

Your puppy's best friend outside your own family unit is his veterinarian. If you don't have one whom you trust or who treated your previous pets, check with your breeder, the local kennel club, or a dog-owning friend you respect.

Any Golden intended for breeding must be screened for hip dysplasia.

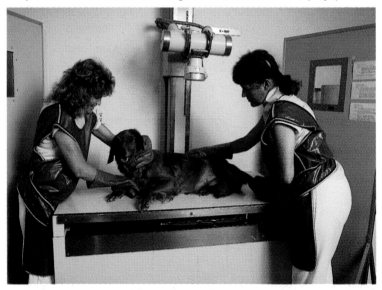

Your Golden puppy should have had at least one puppy shot before he left the breeder.

Today's veterinarians handle more than just routine health care. They can counsel pet owners on breed selection, nutrition, behavior problems, recommend experts on specific health issues and other problems, as well as offer understanding and empathy about your own feelings and concerns.

Before your puppy left his breeder, he should have had at least one series of puppy shots, one or two stool exams and wormings and an examination by a veterinarian for overall

The ears of the Golden Retriever, like those of other drop-eared breeds, are prone to infection. They should be checked on a regular basis for wax build-up and any strong odors.

health and any obvious genetic problems. Heart murmurs, bite and skin problems, eye defects, testicular and other problems can be detected before seven or eight weeks of age.

Arrange an appointment with the veterinarian before you bring your puppy home. Puppy should have a complete health check-up within his first two or three days at home. Most puppy sales, contracts and health guarantees allow for that time frame. Be sure to take along the health records from the breeder.

Also take a sample of your puppy's stool on that first visit. Roundworms, hookworms, tapeworms, whipworms and coccidia are common parasites in puppies, and left untreated, can lead to diarrhea, vomiting and serious weight loss. Your vet will dispense the proper medication to treat the specific parasites that may infest your pup.

Your veterinarian will vaccinate your puppy every two to three weeks until 14 to 16 weeks of age. Keep your own record of the puppy shots and be sure to ask the doctor what they are and what they prevent. The vaccination program should include protection against distemper, hepatitis, leptospirosis (in certain areas), parainfluenza, parvovirus and coronavirus. These are highly contagious diseases, and it's very important that your puppy be fully immunized. Once the puppy has completed his

Puppies should be vaccinated every 2 to 3 weeks until 14 to 16 weeks of age. Be sure to keep your own records and ask your veterinarian which shots he has given and what they prevent.

vaccination schedule, he will need annual booster shots for the above canine diseases, rabies and Lyme disease.

Rabies vaccination can be given at 16 weeks of age, and by law in most states must be given by six months of age, with yearly booster shots thereafter.

Lyme disease has spread to most regions of the United States, although in a few areas there is only minimal risk of Lyme infection. Lyme is transmitted to humans and animals by the tiny deer tick, and the disease can be permanently debilitating. Check with your veterinarian to see if your puppy should be vaccinated against Lyme disease. If you plan to travel with your pup or adult Golden to Lyme-prone areas, be sure to tell your vet.

Heartworm has spread to all areas of

Cattail's Harvest Moon retrieves his puppy bumper.

the United States and Canada, and most veterinarians recommend a heartworm preventative. Heartworm medication comes in liquid and tablet form, and can be given either daily or monthly. A yearly blood test is required to check for the heartworm microfilaria and continue the medication.

Be sure your yard is puppy-proofed before allowing puppy into the garden. This is Polo owned by Andy and Laurie Neff.

Be especially careful about taking your puppy out before he's vaccinated. The stress of a new environment could depress any immunities passed on through the mother, so puppies are especially at risk until they've had a complete series of shots.

Dogs contract many diseases through indirect contact with other dogs' urine and stools, so even walking on busy streets or areas frequented by stray dogs can jeopardize your puppy's health. You can easily carry some contagion into your home on your shoes or clothing, so choose your exercise areas carefully when your Golden is very young and vulnerable.

It's especially important to watch for signs of illness during those first 16 to 20 weeks before immunization is complete. A sudden lack of appetite, diarrhea or bloody stools, frequent urination, vomiting or lethargic behavior can be symptoms of serious illness. If warning signs appear, monitor your puppy's temperature; it can rise rapidly from a normal of 100-101.5°F to 104°F within a very short time. Call your vet if you're suspicious or unsure. Even a 24-hour delay can be fatal for a pup.

Don't become health complacent as your pup matures. Develop a "doggie awareness" and hone it throughout your Golden's lifetime.

When you visit the veterinarian, carry your puppy or keep him on your lap in the waiting room. Don't allow even an adult Golden to wander around the waiting

When sickness strikes, your dog's temperature can rise dramatically within a very short time. It is important that you learn the proper way to take your dog's temperature.

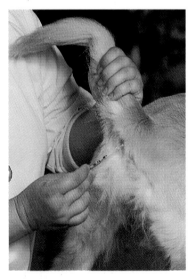

Any change in your Golden's behavior can be cause for concern. Consult your veterinarian at the first sign of illness or abnormal behavior.

room or visit with other dogs. Some of them may be sick or carry fleas...that's why they're at the doctor's! You might even consider waiting in the car to avoid exposing your puppy to infectious animals.

During your initial visits to the veterinarian, be sure to discuss the advantages of spaying your female Golden or neutering your male. These surgical procedures will add to your pet's health as well as control the desire and ability to reproduce. (No, dogs do not have to mate or reproduce to find happiness on this earth. A bitch will

It is wise to keep your Golden leashed whenever he meets a new canine friend.

never miss having a litter of pups, and males do not have to mate in order to fulfill their manhood.) Females spayed before their first heat cycle and males neutered before one year old enjoy a 95 percent reduced risk of certain reproductive cancers and diseases that are major causes of early death in canines.

Additionally, a neutered male will be less dog-aggressive and less apt to go astray in search of romance. A male dog can smell a bitch in heat from impossible distances. (That's real determination!)

A spayed female won't drip estrus fluids all over your floor or carpet or run off looking for a handsome stud dog to cavort with during her semi-annual heat cycle.

The spay and neuter surgical procedures will not affect your Golden's disposition; he or she will still be the silly and lovable beast you know and love. Nor will an altered animal automatically gain weight. Dogs get fat from too much food, food too high in protein or fat content, and/or too little exercise, not from losing their reproductive organs.

While at your veterinarian's office, read any literature or pamphlets on canine disease, parasites, nutrition, dental hygiene, care of older dogs and other health issues displayed as a customer service. Take sample packets home for future reference. A well-informed dog owner will enjoy a healthier canine companion for a longer time.

Your Golden will be a part of your family for a long time. He will need lots of love and the very best care possible.

Feeding Your Puppy

Ask your breeder what kind of food your puppy has been eating and purchase about a week's supply. (Some breeders will send you home with enough food for a day or two. If you plan to change foods, do so in small increments, adding a small amount of the new food to the original over about a week's time, to aid the adjustment. Still your puppy may be off his feed for his first day or two in his new environment but should easily adjust to a regular feeding schedule. Always feed a quality dry puppy food and feed it until he is six months old, then switch to an adult or maintenance formula food. Quality dog food offers a perfectly balanced diet designed specifically for the growing, adult and/or senior dog. Don't add vitamins or supplements like cottage cheese, eggs or other "people" food, as that can cause a nutritional imbalance, which will create problems in the structure of a growing dog as well as contribute to weight and digestive problems in puppies and adult dogs. Dog food is a perfect canine diet designed specifically for canine needs. Unlike people, dogs do not get bored eating the same food everyday.

It's best to avoid generic brands of dog food. Most contain inferior ingredients that are not digestible, may lack proper nutritional content, and can cause loose stools and intestinal upset.

Start your puppy on three meals a day, morning, midday and evening, and increase the portions at each meal in small or quar-

Karl's Lady Taffy dines from food and water bowls set in a raised platform. Some veterinarians encourage the use of food-bowl holders as it prevents deep-chested dogs from gulping their food and thereby wards off bloat.

ter-cup increments whenever he's cleaning his bowl at every meal. Don't use a self-feeding program (leaving food down for the puppy to eat anytime during the day) as that makes it difficult to monitor food intake. It also makes housebreaking difficult because the puppy won't have a regular eating and elimination schedule.

Offer the food dry, with a separate water bowl available, and leave it down for about 20 to 30 minutes. Remove the food bowl even if puppy hasn't eaten every kibble, and don't add additional food at the next meal. Don't worry, he'll catch up later. Eliminate the noon meal at four to five months of age or

sooner if puppy frequently leaves one meal uneaten. Water should be available at all times.

Some puppies have voracious appetites and gobble their food like it's their last meal, while others poke through their food with less enthusiasm. Don't give in and add goodies to the food to perk up a sluggish appetite— that will only foster finicky eating habits.

Watch your puppy's weight and don't let him become over-weight. Overfeeding can cause structural defects in a growing large-breed dog, and many experts now believe it increases the possibility of joint disease in dogs who may be predisposed to

Whether a puppy or an adult, a balanced diet is essential for growth and proper maintenance. Supplementation is discouraged by most breeders and veterinarians.

Classic's Golden Caesar CD owned by Don and Judy Jennings.

hip dysplasia and elbow problems. Some Golden puppies and adults have such thick heavy coats, it's difficult to determine how much of the dog you see is body or simply Golden fur. A good way to check your Golden's weight is to place your hands lightly over the dog's rib cage. You should feel a thin layer of muscle over the ribs and feel the rib cage with very slight pressure of your hands. Chubby puppies may be cute as they waddle about, but overweight pups tend to become overweight adults who tire easily, have health problems, and are more susceptible to heat stroke in hot weather.

Socialization, Play and Puppy Training

A properly raised puppy has received careful and loving handling from birth and will be very trusting. Generous doses of love, intelligent care and consistent attention are the keys to nurturing that well-adjusted pup.

Be gentle when you play with your puppy and take care to avoid

A Golden that has received a generous amount of love and understanding will return that love to his family one-hundredfold. This is Madeline Pantfoeder and Barney.

Camelot's Awesome Illusion owned by Artie Awe in his very own easy chair.

sounds, smells, places and people. For the first few weeks do avoid places such as busy malls, stores or construction sites with loud noises or situations that could startle or frighten him. Puppy should learn to handle extremes on a very gradual basis.

Outdoor walks with your pup in fields or other quiet places can be special bonding times and will teach your puppy to enjoy being with you and to trust you. Encourage him to walk beside you, chat with him and call him to you for a treat or a hug. The time and effort you put in at this early age will reap years of pleasure in a loving and well-adjusted dog, a

picking him up too swiftly or making rapid movements in his direction. As with a baby, anything quick or unexpected can be frightening.

Gradually introduce him to new experiences by taking him with you for exposure to new delightful companion for you, your family and your friends. If you've raised toddlers or teenagers, you'll remember that nothing lasts forever; sadly, neither does puppy-hood.

Research has proven a canine's primary socialization period is from 3 to 16 weeks, meaning that dogs who have not been exposed to humans, other dogs or new situations during this period run a very high risk of growing up fearful of people, other canines and strange

Puppies like to rest in snug places. This is ten-week-old Ripley owned by Suzanne Russ.

A puppy's 8th through 16th week of life is his most critical learning period. This is not, however, a time for formal training.

places. Complete socialization, however, is an ongoing process and must continue throughout the lifetime of the dog to maintain a stable and suitable temperament.

Through further study we also know that a puppy's 8th through 16th weeks are the most critical learning periods of his life. This is not a time for serious formal training. Rather, the pup is "learning to learn," to enjoy the learning process, and to accept you as his new "mom" and pack leader.

In raising and training your puppy, use appropriate levels of expectation. He is, after all, a puppy! The following chart relates the age of puppies to humans, and should remind you to use lots of patience and understanding during your puppy's first year.

make the most of it. It's most important at this age to distinguish between discipline and punishment. You can't punish a pup for behavior that is natural

Puppy Age	Human Age
2 months	2-3 years
4 months	5-7 years
6 months	9-10 years
8 months	13-14 years
10 months	15-16 years

From 8 to 16 weeks a puppy needs closely supervised play and socialization and positive experiences. He is capable of accepting gentle discipline and can understand graduated degrees of obedience training. At this time all training should be play and all play is in effect training so you should

A young Golden Retriever needs closely supervised play and socialization, characterized by positive experiences. Many puppies enjoy having a dog house for a retreat from the world. Make sure it is chew proof!!

All Golden puppies are inquisitive and will inspect everything and everyone they come in contact with. This pup has found a new friend. "Hi there! What's your name?"

to him, behavior over which he has no control, and which has not yet been shaped or molded according to your standards.

Puppies, in fact dogs of any age, also don't understand human anger. If you shout or rail at your spouse or offspring, just watch your dog or puppy shrink away in fear.

WHO you're shouting at is unimportant; the dog is sure it's HIM.

You can help a young puppy learn correct behavior without using actual discipline by distracting him as soon as he gets into mischief. A loud "Ah, ah, ah!" or hand clap can startle the pup and cause him to end the misdeed (drop the slipper, get out of the garbage can) and look to you for direction or attention. Be sure to praise as soon as he stops the behavior and offer a treat, a hug or praise as a reward.

The best course of action at this early age is to keep all temptation (cat food bowls or litter boxes, loose shoes and socks, etc.) away and out of puppy's reach until he outgrows his normal puppy curiosity.

You can often prevent naughty behavior before it begins by anticipating the dog's action. Example: a pound of hamburger lies thawing on the kitchen counter and your dog lingers nearby with both eyes glued on the package

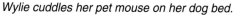

Wylie cuddles her pet mouse on her dog bed.

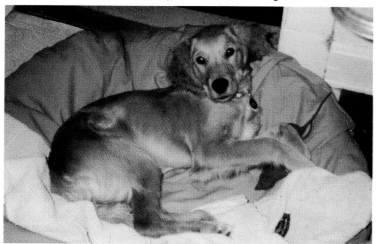

of meat. You know instantly what he's thinking. You can be just as effective by warning him with a firm "Ah, ah, ah!" or "No, no, no!" You've read his mind, redirected his thinking and reshaped his behavior without suffering the consequences of misbehavior. This type of positive behavior shaping avoids the use of negatives and helps create a confident attitude in your pup.

When puppies do need discipline, however, there exists a variety of effective methods to help your puppy understand what behavior you want him to stop. Remember, timing is the most important element in any type of discipline. The disciplinary action must occur while the puppy is actually performing the undesirable behavior; tugging on your pants leg, chewing your best shoe, etc.

When puppy misbehaved within the litter, it took but a single word, a snarl, from mother to stop him in his tracks. As his new pack leader, you too can use a growl, a low "Grrrr," as an effective means of stopping inappropriate behavior. When he stops, be sure to praise profusely! If he persists, a scruff-shake may be in order; after all, his mother used it with success.

Meet Golden Thunder, bred by the author, owned and adored by the Cal Zimmerman family.

This is Karl's Lady Taffy, owned by Karl Baumwell, with her Nylafloss®.

On small pups, grasp the scruff of the neck and the collar with one hand and shake briskly and briefly, just a gentle shake or two while barely raising his front feet off the floor. Larger or older pups may require both hands, placed on each side of the neck. Be sure to maintain solid eye contact during the shake and use a growl or firm "No!" His memories of mama should jolt him into good behavior.

Ignoring puppy for misbehavior can also be effective, but it must be immediate and clear to the pup. Goldens especially are very social animals and will be most unhappy if they're isolated from pack members. When puppy nips at your fingertips or toes, say "OOUUUUCH" in a sharp voice, then immediately turn away from the pup and fold your arms. Wait a minute, not too long, then turn and hug and praise the pup who is now NOT chewing on your hand. If he begins anew, ignore him once again, until the realization sets in that nipping will cost him your attention and companionship.

As retrievers, Goldens are considered "oral" dogs who love to carry something ... anything!...in their mouths. Not only their toys or chew bones, but your socks and slippers, dish towels, your son's stuffed teddy bear, even your hand if it's available. Your puppy must learn what objects he may and may not retrieve and carry about. It's best to GO TO the

Frisbee®* has proven to be one of the Golden Retriever's favorite sports. *The trademark Frisbee is used under license from Mattel, Inc., California, USA.

The Gumabone® Frisbee®* is soft, pliable, and can easily be picked up by your Golden Retriever because it has a bone molded on the top of the disk. *The trademark Frisbee is used under license from Mattel, Inc., California, USA.

"Mouthing" and nipping are the most difficult of Golden puppy problems. Chewing is normal for pups of every breed, even more instinctive for a Golden. Pups have difficulty under-standing the difference between what they may and may not chew. Often pups will chew our hands and we allow it because it doesn't hurt. Later when it smarts, we say "No!" and totally con-fuse the pup. The key is not to allow it to begin with.

Jumping up is a problem similar to chewing and persists well beyond the chew-ing stage! Pups are conditioned from a very early age that jumping up is accept-

puppy when he has a forbidden object, re-move it gently and praise him for releas-ing it, then immediately offer him a puppy toy instead. Never allow a game of tug-of-war and always discourage the instinct to "hold" or mouth your hand.

able behavior...they stand on their hind legs to peer over the top of their whelping box, they do the same at puppy gates. In their enthusiasm to greet visitors, they jump up and are rewarded with a hearty scoop into loving arms.

Seven, eight or nine weeks later we attempt to reverse that behavior, one that is not only instinctive but has been ingrained as acceptable. As with chewing, your patience may be tested. Don't give up...puppies do grow up and out of

Socialization is very important. If a puppy is improperly socialized, or not socialized at all, it will never reach its full potential as a suitable family companion. For a Golden, this is the greatest disappointment of all!

such behavior...with your help.

If at all possible, attend a puppy class. Age requirements vary according to class health requirements; puppies are often accepted from 12 weeks of age. It's important for puppy to have at least one adult shot before entering a class to protect him against exposure to infection and disease.

Puppy classes expose the "students" to social situations with their peers and provide a variety of experiences to teach them to be unafraid and unthreatened by new or unusual situations; open umbrellas, boards to straddle and jump over, objects to step on and walk over. Pups also learn to walk on a loose leash, and to accept some degree of physical restraint to prepare for future training, grooming and veterinary examination.

Some classes also take you and your puppy through basic obedience commands;

Four-month-old pup in puppy class with author. A puppy learns to sit with treats and lots of praise.

A puppy class is a wonderful way to provide a variety of experiences to your Golden and teach it to be unafraid and unthreatened by new or unusual situations.

sit, stay, heel, down and come. You should continue through the next level of a basic or novice obedience class at a rate comfortable for both you and the dog and compatible with his learning ability. A well-behaved Golden is a pleasure to live with and a welcome addition in most social situations. Most dog owners can't produce such an animal without formal obedience instruction.

Complete instruction on puppy and obedience training is beyond the scope of this book. There are many excellent books available that are dedicated solely to puppy training instruction, and a wise owner makes use

A puppy must spend time with his dam, his littermates and humans to develop into a well-balanced adult dog.

The quality of your adult Golden's behavior will be in direct proportion to the amount of time you spend training him during puppyhood. Becky and her young Golden protégé, Pardner, show off their ribbons.

A Golden Retriever puppy needs personal attention during his formative weeks in order to develop a confident, outgoing personality. Responsible breeders spend much time socializing each and every puppy. The author spends countless hours with her litter of 12 pups.

of more than one. If you make the most of this vital period in your puppy's growth, you can obtain maximum results from your efforts and your pup. The first 16 to 20 weeks are critical...you can't reclaim this time after your pup has grown. The quality of your adult Golden's behavior will be in direct proportion to the amount of time you spend training him during his puppyhood.

Check with your vet, your breeder, or local dog club to find a puppy class and future obedience classes in your area.

Grooming

Goldens are often referred to as "easy keepers," a misleading and almost contradictory term. "Easy" means they require only basic (but regular!) grooming and need no surgical alterations to the ears or tail. Regular means once or twice a week, if the owner wants to avoid a delicate layer of Golden fur on their pillow and dinner plate. A Golden's double coat is "self-cleaning"; however, brushing will remove

Your Golden Retriever's coat will need grooming once or twice a week, more if he enjoys splashing in puddles or ponds.

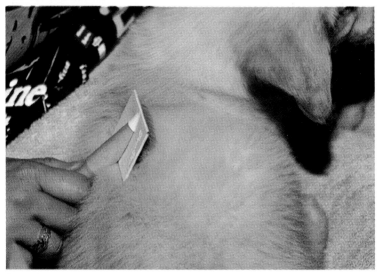

Puppies gradually learn to accept grooming. Accustom your Golden pup to being groomed at a young age so he will enjoy it as an adult.

dried mud and other dirt—the key word here is "brushing."

Puppies gradually learn to love the grooming process, with the emphasis on "gradually." Keep early sessions short, perhaps only a few brush strokes. Slowly increase the length of time and the amount of handling. Always praise him lavishly when he stands and cooperates. Tell him he's wonderful and beautiful, that you love him to pieces, and he'll discover these are the best of times. Use this time also to remind him you're the pack leader by demanding he stand still for a few moments. It's easier to teach control to a 10-pound pup than to the 70-pound adult you'll be brushing a year from now.

Proper grooming equipment includes a pin-brush, slicker brush, steel comb with wide and narrow-spaced teeth, a nail clipper and a pair of canine grooming scissors.

About 10 to 15 minutes of brushing twice a week will keep an adult Golden coat shining and free of mats and tangles. Use a pin-brush or slicker brush to remove dead hair from the under-coat and stimulate the oil glands.

Following a pattern makes the job easier on both you and the dog. Starting at the dog's rear, work on the coat in small sections at a time, "parting" the coat all the way to the skin. Use one hand to hold the hair back, and with the other hand, run the brush from the skin outward through the hair. Continue in sequential

This puppy will definitely need a bath! China jumped into the pond and discovered there was mud underneath that water! ("But it sure was fun!")

Frequent brushing will keep your Golden's coat free of mats and tangles.

during periods of heavy shedding.

Brushing is the best time to remove mats, the knobs of tangled and dead hair that often form around the ears and tail and under the arms. A slicker brush or special mat rake can be used to work through the mat without leaving a damaged or flat spot in the hair. A straight-across scissors cut will leave unsightly lines in the coat.

Use this grooming time to examine your dog for fleas, ticks and skin irritations. Roll him over to check his underside for tiny dark flecks of flea dirt that turn reddish-brown when moistened. Don't let your puppy resist

sections, always working upwards and forwards. Be careful not to abrade the dog's skin while brushing. A steel comb with wide- and narrow-spaced teeth or a shedding comb are more efficient grooming tools when you roll him over. Insist he submit to this process to remind him you're the boss.

If you suspect fleas, follow your veterinarian's advice on flea control, not only on the dog but also on his bedding and throughout your house and yard. Use extreme caution when using any flea products. They can cause minor allergic responses that can escalate to fatal toxic reactions if products are improperly used or incompatible ingredients combined.

While brushing, also check for rashes, "hot spots" and other skin problems. Some Goldens are allergic to fleas, molds, and certain plants including grass, while others seem predisposed to minor skin irritations. Allergic reactions can include rashes, redness, itching and swelling.

Hot spots, a skin condition common to Goldens, are raw open sores on the skin, often hidden under a heavy coat. Left untreated

Don't forget the legs. The feathering on the back of the legs should be included in your grooming sessions.

In the summer months, your Golden Retriever will enjoy water sports with the kids. Wading pools make excellent substitute bathtubs too!

they spread rapidly and can cause the dog great discomfort. The area is sometimes shaved to enhance the healing process, as it must remain dry in order to properly heal. Dogs will often gnaw and chew at the affected area. Check with your veterinarian for proper treatment if you discover hot spots on your Golden.

Also check your dog's ears during routine grooming sessions. Remove any brown waxy material from the outer ear flap with a cottonball moistened with hydrogen peroxide. Use an ear cleansing agent to clean accumulated wax from the ear canal. Consult your vet if you discover a persistent or runny discharge or bad odor from the ear. Other trouble signs are frequent scratching at the ears and frequent shaking of the head.

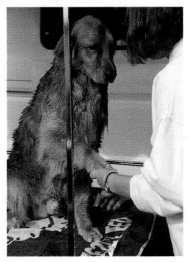

Feet and nails are the least popular areas to groom. Most dogs dislike nail trimming, but if you start the habit with your pup, your dog should learn to tolerate the process without a fuss.

Feet and nails are the least popular areas to groom. Most dogs dislike nail trimming, but if you start the habit with your pup, your dog should learn to tolerate the process without a fuss. A puppy's nails should be trimmed often so he won't scratch his human family during playtime. Your puppy will most likely resist, and initially you may have to settle for one foot per trimming session. Don't be overly demanding, but do insist that he cooperate.

Use a good quality nail clipper and ask your vet or an experienced friend to demonstrate the process on your dog. Be careful to avoid cutting the quick, the pink vein area of the nail, as it will bleed. In those Goldens with black nails, cut only the hooked part of the nail, near the tip. A flashlight placed beneath the nail will often reveal the faint pink line of the quick.

About once a month, after trimming the dog's nails, clip the hair around the feet and between the pads, cutting it level with the bottom of the pads. Hair on the underside of the foot collects mud, burrs and ice balls, which is uncomfortable for the dog. For the fastidious Golden owner, trimmed feet will also track less mud, snow and ice into the house.

Dental care need not be difficult or unpleasant if you start it early in the puppy-grooming game. Dental plaque build-up is responsible for many infections and internal diseases in adult and senior dogs, as the bacteria enter the dog's system through the affected gumlines. Weekly tooth brushing with canine dental products will keep tartar build-up to a minimum. (Human dental products can actually harm a dog.) Dry dog foods and chew products such as Nylabone® and Gumabone® will also help maintain healthy teeth and gums.

Your Golden Retriever's dental health is important. Provide him with plenty of safe chew devices such as the Gumabone® Frisbee®* *The trademark Frisbee in used under license from Mattel Inc., California, USA.

Exercise

As sporting dogs, Goldens require regular exercise to maintain physical and mental fitness. Most Goldens are high energy animals who love and need to run, and who can become mis-chievously destructive if they are bored or physically unchallenged. They should be walked daily, according to the individual dog's stamina and desire. A fenced-in backyard will not provide adequate

Goldens love and need to run. Even a puppy requires enough room to run and play to get the proper exercise.

exercise for your dog. YOU are the dog's motivation to play, run and have fun. A frequent game of catch with a tennis ball or Frisbee, flyball or other energetic canine activity will keep your dog and yourself in shape and entertained. Most Goldens are natural retrievers who will happily cooperate in games of fetch, and a hefty daily dozen will help keep the average dog in shape. Hikes and bicycle rides, romps in the park or on the beach are traditional fun activities for athletic retrievers. Be creative...and your dog will be less likely to create his own outlets for excess energy.

Most Goldens love to play a game of catch with their owners.

Be extra cautious, however, about exercising your Golden off leash in public places. Even the most reliable dog can surprise you by chasing a rabbit or squirrel in the middle of a game of catch, often across a busy street. A dog or puppy

Exercise your Golden before beginning a training session. If he runs off a little steam, he'll concentrate better on his lessons.

may decide to run after a child or other dog and in seconds will be out of sight. Don't risk losing your Golden. A leashed dog is seldom a statistic.

If you plan to hunt with your Golden or train for obedience or agility trials, you'll need a regular exercise program to maintain the physical fitness and endurance essential to these sporting disciplines. Combine your training and exercise routines...add some fun activities like ball tossing to relieve the stress of training while you build and shape your Golden athlete. Your dog's good health is more than just a bonus for your efforts.

Hereditary Diseases

All purebred dogs are susceptible to certain hereditary diseases that are common to their particular breed, and Goldens are no exception. As popularity increases with any breed of dog, unfortunately so does indiscriminate breeding, which then raises the incidence of hereditary diseases. Hip dysplasia and eye diseases head the list of several hereditary

Chances R Mollie's Geronimo bred by the author and loved and missed by owner Phillip Bauer.

This is Wiekse Veld a puppy from Denmark, owned by Henri and Thea Dekkers.

health problems that plague today's Golden Retriever.

HIP DYSPLASIA (HD)

Hip dysplasia simply means poor development of the hip joint. While a severe case can affect a working dog's capacity to perform, even a mild case can cause painful arthritis in the average house dog. Reliable breeders x-ray the hips of their breeding stock to screen for this disease. The x-rays are evaluated by the Orthopedic Foundation for Animals (OFA) and dogs with clear hips are issued an OFA certificate. The OFA number will also appear on the dog's AKC registration.

Dogs must be at least two years old before their hips are considered fully mature and eligible for a permanent OFA number.

A dysplastic dog should never be used for breeding. A pedigree with several generations of cleared hips is the best insurance that your puppy will not be affected by this disease.

A second method to screen canines for HD has been developed at the University of Pennsylvania School of Veterinary Medicine. Known as the PennHIP, this technique also uses x-rays, but measures hip joint laxity and can be used on dogs as young as 16 weeks of age. Over 100 PennHIP centers have been established throughout North America to screen for susceptibility to hip dysplasia.

ELBOW DYSPLASIA (ED) AND OSTEOCHONDRITIS (OCD)

In 1990 OFA created a second registry to provide a data base for dogs to certify they are free of several forms of elbow and shoulder problems.

Like hip dysplasia, ED and OCD are developmental diseases of the joints and are the major cause of front-end lameness in many large breeds of dogs. The symptoms occur most often in the growing dog, usually in recurring lameness which can range from mild to severe. The problems can be diagnosed only through x-ray. The OFA number of elbow-cleared dogs will appear on their AKC registration. Affected dogs should be removed from breeding programs.

EYE DISEASES

Goldens have several hereditary eye problems, including hereditary cataracts and progressive retinal atrophy (PRA), which is a progressive deterioration of the retina or light-receptor area of the eye that may result in complete blindness. Only a board-certified veterinary ophthalmologist can determine if a dog is free of eye disease. Dogs that have been properly examined and cleared can be registered with the Canine Eye Registry Foundation (CERF), which will issue a numbered certificate of clearance. Eyes must be examined annually until the dog is eight years of age, as certain forms of eye disease can occur up to that time. Dogs with hereditary cataracts or PRA should never be used for breeding purposes.

Several less serious eye problems with eyelids and eyelashes may also occur in Goldens. While some of these can be corrected surgically, they render the dog ineligible for the show ring, and those dogs with problems of a hereditary nature should not be bred.

HYPOTHYROIDISM

This is a malfunction of the thyroid gland with symptoms that include obesity, lethargy, coat problems, reproductive problems and sterility. The disease can be diagnosed only through laboratory tests, which measure the T3 and T4 levels of thyroid serum in the blood. Affected dogs can often be successfully treated

This is Malcairn's Firebrand Folly CD owned by Sally Jenkins.

Be sure to provide shade and protection from the ultra-violet rays for your Golden on a hot summer day. This is Dusty, owned by Janet Edmonds taking a sunbath.

with medication, but experts recommend that dogs who require medication be eliminated from a breeding program.

EPILEPSY

Epilepsy is a neurological disorder caused by abnormal electrical patterns in the brain. Recurring seizures can be inherited or may be caused by a number of environmental factors, including viral and infectious disease, chemical imbalance, nutritional imbalance, toxic reaction, and trauma. Today's Golden is among a dozen breeds predisposed to hereditary epilepsy, with the initial onset occurring most often from six months to three years of age. Although the mode of inheritance has not yet been determined, dogs with recurring seizures should not be bred, and some experts suggest further that parents and siblings of seizuring dogs also be removed from breeding programs.

Veterinarian Tim Pennington gets a grateful lick after he put a cast on this pup's broken leg.

SUBVALVULAR AORTIC STENOSIS

This inherited heart defect is known to affect some lines or families of Golden Retrievers. The disease is caused by a stricture in the left ventricle, which restricts the blood flow out of the heart and can lead to sudden and unexpected death after normal to heavy activity. SAS can be detected by a board-

KC's Chances R Walkin' on Sunshine, CD, MH, WCX, TDI owned by the author.

VON WILLEBRAND'S DISEASE

The Golden Retriever is one of 54 breeds known to be affected with vWD, a form of thyroid disease which can lead to hypothyroidism. VWD is an inherited bleeding disorder, similar to hemophilia in humans. Problems from excessive bleeding can occur during surgery or from something as minor as a cut quick during routine nail clipping. All breeding stock should have a blood test to identify dogs who carry the vWD trait, and affected dogs should never be bred.

certified veterinary cardiologist as early as eight to 16 weeks of age. Dogs should be reevaluated at 12 and 24 months of age, and all dogs should be cleared before they are considered for a breeding program.

More detailed information on the hereditary diseases that affect Golden Retrievers may be obtained from the national parent club.

Activities for Golden Retrievers

Goldens are natural "everything" dogs who love to work and please their humans. They are one of the few breeds today capable of participating in almost every canine activity offered by kennel clubs and other dog organizations. This chapter will give you only a brief overview of the sporting world available to you and your Golden. Information

The Golden Retriever is one of the few breeds capable of participating in almost every canine activity offered by dog organizations. This is Chances R Wizard of Wonders UD, WCX with his happy 16-year-old owner-trainer Bridget Carlsen.

and instruction on training for these activities is too vast for the confines of this book. If you're interested in any particular aspect of Golden activity, read several books devoted to the subject and consult breeders and experts who regularly participate in these activities. Your Golden will be more than ready when you are!

SHOWING YOUR GOLDEN

If you've purchased your Golden with hopes or intentions of showing him in conformation, you already understand that dogs in the breed ring are judged against other

This is Westben's Might Tango winning Best of Breed in the Fayetteville Kennel Club.

BEST OF
BREED OR VARIETY

FAYETTEVILLE
KENNEL CLUB
MAR
1969
THE STANDARD IMAGE
CHUCK TATHAM

dogs. The winning dog (male) and bitch (female) are awarded points toward their championship in accordance with the number of dogs defeated. A total of 15 points, including two "major" wins of three or more points, is required to become a bench Champion, with a maximum of five points awarded at any single show.

Dogs are judged on their physical structure (head, teeth, feet, bone structure, muscle tone, etc.), gait (as observed from the front, side and rear), physical condition (i.e., weight, muscle and coat condition), and on animation and temperament (outgoing and confident, shy or aggressive, etc.).

Conformation dogs

Sunclad Streaker's Jupiter UD owned by Barbara Branstad.

compete in any of six regular classes, with the winner of each class competing in a final class. Dogs and bitches are judged separately, with the males judged first.

1. *Puppy*—for dogs and bitches between 6 and 12 months of age. These classes may be further divided into 6 to 9 month and 9 to 12 month classes.

2. *12-18 month class*—at specialty shows only. Specialties are shows held for any one specific breed.

3. *Novice*—for dogs and bitches that have never won a first place in a class other than puppy or novice.

4. *Bred by Exhibitor*—for dogs and bitches except champions, owned and exhibited by the same person or kennel who is also the recognized breeder of record with AKC.

5. *American bred*—for dogs and bitches bred and born in the U.S.A.

6. *Open*—for all dogs and bitches, American and foreign bred.

In the Winners class, the winners of all of the above classes compete for Winners Dog and Winners Bitch. A non-point award is also given to Reserve Winners Dog and Reserve Winners Bitch, in the event the winning dog is found to be ineligible to receive the award and its accompanying points.

Into the final level of breed competition come the Winners Dog and Winners Bitch to compete for Best of Winners. The Winners Dog and Winners Bitch then go on to compete with champions for Best of Breed and Best of Opposite Sex.

Many kennel clubs

offer conformation classes where you and your Golden can gain ring experience and learn more about gaiting and grooming for the breed ring. To obtain a copy of the AKC Rules Applying to Registration and Dog Shows, write AKC, 51 Madison Ave., New York, NY 10010.

OBEDIENCE TRIALS

Have you noticed a smiling Golden face seems to dominate TV

Here's "Baby Face." Goldenbear's Hotsy Totsy taking Group First Puppy with breeder-owner Cindy Lichtenberger.

GROUP
FIRST
PUPPY
LEHIGH VALLEY
KENNEL CLUB
JANUARY
1989   DAVE ASHBEY

commercials, newspaper and magazine ads and other product promotions? The modern Golden Retriever has no doubt been trained to sell more cars, boats and dog food than any other breed of dog.

Small wonder then that the breed dominates the obedience ring, where the ultimate in trainability is required. As natural pleasers and willing workers, Goldens thrive on "team" sports like obedience where they can work closely with their owners. For the past two decades the eager Golden Retriever has consistently led all other breeds in obedience competition.

In obedience trials, dogs are judged not on appearance, but on their performance in a set of regulated obedience exercises. The sport is open to all registered breeds of dogs and offers three classes or levels of competition: Novice, Open and Utility. Dogs who qualify in each class earn "legs" that apply to the respective titles at each level. Three legs (or three qualifying scores of at least 170 points out of a possible 200) will earn the Novice dog the title of Companion Dog (CD), the Open dog the title of Companion Dog Excellent (CDX) and the Utility dog, a Utility Dog (UD) title. The title of UDX was added by AKC in 1993

Chances R This Bud's For Me, "Buddy" at four months of age, was already at attention on a sit/stay. Owner, Lois Busse.

to offer added incentive to those people who want to continue showing their dogs in obedience competition, but are unable to pursue or attain the title of Obedience Trial Champion (OTC). A UDX is awarded to UD dogs who obtain qualifying scores in both the Open and Utility classes at ten separate obedience trials.

All obedience classes include a heeling exercise, on and off lead, and in Utility, heeling without verbal assistance. Dogs in Novice and Open must sit and

Am. Can. OTCh. Splashdown Tess of Culynwood WCX (OD), owned by DeeDee and Billy Anderson, proudly displays one of her many awards.

lie down for varying lengths of time, with and without the owners present. Advanced classes include retrieving exercises, high and broad jumps, scent discrimination, and non-verbal hand signals. An obedience Golden prancing in the ring with its eyes riveted on its owner is usually cause for applause at most obedience trials.

Eileen Robinson training Thornfield's Mister Mario CD.

There are many good books on training for obedience competition available for the serious obedience fancier. It is also best to attend formal obedience training classes and several "fun" or practice matches before entering an obedience trial. You should also be completely familiar with the AKC rules. The *Rules and Regulations for Obedience Competition* may be requested from the AKC, 51 Madison Ave., New York, NY 10010.

TRACKING

The Golden Retriever's nose is one of its most famous parts. It is, after all, the quality that led Lord Tweedmouth to outcross his yellow retrievers to a Bloodhound to enhance the offspring's scenting ability.

Although tracking is a relative of obedience trials, it involves the dog's ability to use its nose. The dog must follow the scent or path of a person across hedgerow and field, and find the glove, wallet or object left by the tracklayer at the end of the path or track.

Tracking is a skill often used in canine

The very talented and versatile U-UD, Am. Can. OTCh. Beckwiths Hennessy Five Star UDTX, WCX, Can. WC, owned by Nancy Light, practicing scent discrimination for the Utility ring.

Goldens love to swim...for pleasure and play as well as in field competition.

service to mankind, and tracking tests demonstrate not only a dog's ability but also his willingness and pleasure in the performance of that work. Similar to obedience, the tests are conducted on a pass-fail basis.

To earn the TD (Tracking Dog) title, a dog must follow a 440- to 500-yard track, which includes at least two right-angle turns on a track that is 30 minutes to 2 hours old, and retrieve the glove or wallet dropped at the track's end. The TDX (Tracking Dog Excellent) dog faces a more difficult course with more complex terrain over 800 to

1,000 yards long, with five to seven turns and the track being three to five hours old. The dog must locate and retrieve four articles left by the tracklayer along the way, generally a scarf, shoe, sock or hat, with the last article being a wallet or glove.

Tracking buffs who have participated in other areas of dog competition proclaim tracking to be the most exhilarating of any person-dog team sport. The handler must have complete faith in his dog's ability to follow the track, and the dog must sense that trust. If you have confidence in your Golden's nose, try tracking. You'll enjoy it as much as he will!

A copy of the manual on *Tracking Regulations* can be obtained from the American Kennel Club in New York. Books on tracking, training methods and how to get started are also available at bookstores, pet stores and in dog-supply catalogs.

FIELD TRIALS AND HUNTING TESTS: THE DIFFERENCE

The basic difference between the retriever field trial and a hunting test is competition. In hunting tests the dogs are judged against a standard of performance and either pass or fail. Field trial dogs, however, are judged against the other dogs' performances and eliminated

The author's girl, China has succeeded in many areas of canine competition including obedience and field work.

when the quality of their work falls below those dogs. With an average of 50 to 100 entries in a major stake that carries championship points, and only four placements, it's easy to see why field trials are called a "loser's game."

AKC retriever field trials consist of four stakes: the minor stakes consist of Derby, for dogs under two years of age, and Qualifying, for intermediate dogs who are trained to a moderate level of proficiency and haven't yet won or placed in a major stake. The two major stakes include the Amateur, for amateur handlers only, offering points toward an Amateur Field Championship (AFC) title, and Open, which offers points toward a Field Championship (FC) title and is open to both professional and amateur handlers.

Derby dogs are tested on double retrieves on land and in the water. Handling is not allowed (directing the dog to a bird with hand signals) and the emphasis is on a young dog's natural ability.

Can. OTCh. Hickory Dickory Zachary UDT, JH, WC, clears the bar with spectacular style. Owner, Andrea Johnson.

Qualifying dogs generally face triple retrieves and single blind retrieves (where handling is required) on land and in water. This is the mid-level work for the field trial dog.

The Amateur and Open stakes involve multiple retrieves on land and in water, often at distances exceeding 300 yards. Distractions and complex terrain add to the degree of difficulty, and a superb level of training is required to complete these tests.

Competition in field trials is fierce. Most competing dogs have had some degree of professional training, and it's difficult for the beginner to be successful without a lot of luck

KC's Sparkle Plenty MH, WCX, and owner Kaye Fuller D.V.M., sporting happy smiles after the qualifying win which earned Sparkle's All-Age status.

and a truly spectacular animal. If you're interested in this aspect of retrieverdom, be sure to attend a few trials and ask a lot of questions. Some professional trainers offer seminars on various levels of training. Books on training

OTCh. Meadowpond Especial One UDT, SH, WCX waits for the ducks to fall with owner Glenda Brown.

and trialing are also helpful. Try to join a training group who will help you train and work with your dog. If you're willing to drive your vehicle through bumpy fields and throw birds and bumpers in the rain and other nasty weather, you'll be a welcome addition to most training groups.

The AKC hunting tests were designed for the non-competitive sportsman who wanted to pursue field work with the family retriever who may or may not be a hunting companion. The tests consist of three stakes designed to test a dog's natural abilities on graduated levels of difficulty.

The Junior Hunter (JH) title requires four qualifying scores or "legs." Dogs must complete two single retrieves on land and two in water at a maximum of 100 yards. The Senior Hunter (SH) needs five legs, four if he already has a JH. The Senior dog must complete more difficult double retrieves on land and in water, do single land and water blinds (birds the dog has not seen shot) and honor

It was a good day in the field for pheasant hunter Chances R This Bud's For Me, owned by Lois Busse.

HRCh. Holway Vodka owned by Mercedes Hitchcock leaps into the water with spectacular style and drive.

another working dog (remain steady while other dog retrieves). A Master Hunter (MH) needs six legs to earn the title, five if he has an SH. He must complete multiple land and water and combined land-water retrieves, do multiple blind retrieves on land and in water,

honor, and work under more difficult and complex conditions.

In all three stakes, dogs must retrieve ducks or pheasants on land and ducks in water. All dogs are judged against a standard of performance and are not eliminated because another dog had better work.

Because hunting tests are non-competitive, the atmosphere is more relaxed and friendly, with the participants more supportive of the other handlers. The rapid rise in the popularity of the hunting tests hopefully will result in breeding more "retriever" into the Golden Retriever of the future.

For complete information, rules and

guidelines on these two AKC retriever activities, you can request *Regulations and Guidelines for AKC Hunting Tests for Retrievers* and/or *Standard Procedure for AKC Retriever Field Trials* from AKC at 51 Madison Ave., New York, NY 10010. The United Kennel Club (UKC) and the North American Hunting Retriever Association (NAHRA) also conduct hunt tests for dogs who are registered with their organizations.

Ready to go again, Haven Farms Just Do It Nike CD, TD, JH, WC, owned by Susan Hawxhurst.

This Golden returns and sits to deliver the bird for owner-trainer Roger Fuller.

WORKING CERTIFICATE TESTS

Working Certificate tests are non-competitive field events designed by the Golden Retriever Club of America to demonstrate and encourage the instincts and natural abilities of the Golden Retriever in the field. If your Golden is a retrieve-a-holic, if he loves to hunt a little or a lot, the GRCA Working Certificate (WC) and Working Certificate Excellent (WCX) tests can offer an opportunity to work as a team with your Golden and give your dog a chance to do what he was originally bred to do—retrieve birds instead of a Frisbee® or a tennis ball.

The WC/WCX tests were devised to evaluate the retriever's natural ability in the field; marking (watch a bird go down, remember where it fell and retrieve it), his intelligence, perseverance (keep hunting until he finds the bird), nose (how well he uses his scenting ability to locate the bird), his style and desire to retrieve, and to a minimal degree, his trainability. Dogs are tested on land and in water. They are judged against a standard and not expected to perform at or near the level of the field trial or hunting test retriever.

The WC consists of a double retrieve on land and two short single retrieves in the water. A WCX requires the dog to complete a triple retrieve on land, a double in the water and an honoring test (to remain steady while another dog works).

WC/WCX tests are hosted by GRCA member clubs and open to all AKC-registered Goldens. Most clubs hold practice sessions before the test and often offer training assistance to newcomers as well as old timers. Complete rules and regulations are available from the GRCA secretary. You can direct inquiries to the GRCA columnist, c/o AKC, 51 Madison Ave., New York, NY 10010.

Chances R Mein Leibschen CDX, WC owned by the author.

Most agility clubs provide specialized training equipment so both dog and owner can participate in this fun sport.

AGILITY

Does your Golden love to climb the slide at the neighborhood park? Does he sail effortlessly over the log pile, leap over your head for his Frisbee®, straddle the porch rail after a squirrel? He might be a natural for agility!

The excitement and frantic activity of the agility course has transformed the sport from a spectator event at obedience trials during the 1980s into a popular sporting event today. Its popularity stems from the frenetic pace of the dog's racing through a complex course of obstacles to jump over, crawl into or under, straddle, cross over, balance on or weave through. The dog masters the obstacles, he goes faster, and the excitement mounts with every leap and turn.

Open to both purebred and mixed-breed dogs, agility attracts competitors from every corner of dogdom. While some breeds are not physically suited to the sport, the athletic Golden Retriever is a natural for the demands of the agility course.

In 1986 the United States Dog Agility Association (USDAA) was founded as the governing umbrella organization. Over 17 member clubs across the country sponsor licensed agility compe-

At six months old, Chances R Kirby, owned by Debbie Stremke, discovered the thrills of agility competition.

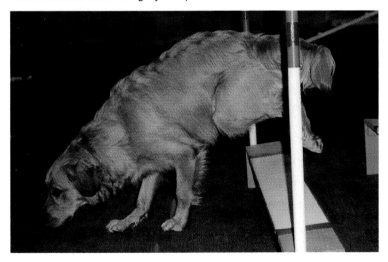

titions. Their membership, however, includes non-competitive agility enthusiasts who just want to have fun with their dogs.

In 1994 AKC welcomed Dog Agility into its official ranks. Accomplished agility dogs can earn titles that will appear as a suffix after their registered names.

The Rules and Regulations for Agility Trials can be obtained from AKC at 51 Madison Ave., New York, NY 10010.

In 1994 the Trans-National Club for Dog Agility, INC (NCDA) and UKC joined forces to offer another version of agility tests. For more information, write

Moorelake Crosby's American Dream coming off the teeter-totter at an agility trial.

Glorybee Darling Dundee UD performing in Novice agility.

to UKC, 100 E. Kilgore Rd., Kalamazoo, MI 49001.

Many kennel clubs also have agility equipment and classes or committees to encourage participation. All handlers and dogs who have tried agility proclaim the same motto "Try it, you'll like it!"

Teaching Your Golden Puppy to Retrieve

If you have visions of your Golden's tearing through the field after a pheasant or swimming across a pond to retrieve a duck, you will need a Golden who has been bred for that purpose. Unfortunately the division within the breed has produced many lines of Goldens who have little interest in hunting or retrieving. If you own a Golden who dislikes birds or refuses to retrieve feathers with enthusiasm, love and enjoy your dog for all

Puppies can learn to retrieve in the water at a very early age.

Nine-week-old "China" challenges her brother for the training bumper.

its many other fine qualities, but don't expect it to fill your bird sack, win field trials or excel at hunting tests. If your field-type Golden dream persists, you might consider purchasing a field-bred Golden, now or later, to take into the field.

If field work is in your puppy's future, be careful when doling out discipline if he "retrieves" your underwear or shoes. While he must learn the rules about what objects he is allowed to retrieve and carry about, you still want to encourage his desire to return to you after he retrieves. It's best then to *go to* the puppy when he has a forbidden object, remove it gently and praise him for releasing it, then immediately offer him a puppy toy instead. Never allow a game of tug-of-war and always discourage the instinct to "hold" or mouth your hand.

When teaching young Goldens the retrieving game, whether as a hunting or hunt test partner or field trial competitor, the basics are the same: you must maintain a high level of enthusiasm at all times. The objective is to build desire in a retriever pup by fortifying it with fun and success.

Never give a puppy more than three retrieves at one time, less if his desire wanes. Always quit when he's still charged up and straining to retrieve once more. A good analogy is the child who is given an unlimited amount of ice cream every day. Within a short time the child will tire of ice cream and look for something else. Restrict that treat to a single tablespoon a day, and soon the child will tremble with excitement at the mere sight of the ice cream container. So it is also with puppies and retrieving.

One or two sessions of two or three short retrieves a day will give most pups a good start. Use a puppy bumper or an old sock stuffed with other socks, with possibly a pigeon wing fastened to the sock with tape. This training tool is to be used for training only, *never* as a toy or everyday plaything. Make sure your kids and well-meaning relatives follow that rule to the letter.

Begin by waving the bumper in front of the puppy's nose to get him eager and excited. Toss the bumper a few feet while holding the puppy, then release him while it's in mid-air. Don't throw the bumper very high, rather throw "sliders" at puppy's eye level at this age, since a seven- or eight-week-old puppy has limited

Be sure your Golden puppy knows what he is looking for before he sets out on a retrieve. A stuffed sock makes a good training bumper for a very young pup.

With a proper introduction to water, a Golden will learn to love swimming and doing anything wet.

it gently, still with praise, and toss again. A good place to begin this exercise is a long hallway, so puppy has nowhere to run with the bumper except back to you. Start short and gradually increase the distance the entire length of the hallway. Be sure the bumper is highly visible on the carpet or flooring.

Once you move outdoors with his retrieving, start on short cut grass and back up to very short distances again, as you are now adding other variables or distractions to his retrieving environment. As with most aspects of dog training, when introducing anything new, it's best to back up to a

peripheral vision and can't track objects that move laterally or up and down too rapidly. Tell pup to "Fetch it up" or "Go get it." Praise and encourage him to return to you, then hug and praise him again *while he's still holding the bumper* in his mouth. Remove point where you can assure the dog or puppy of success.

When working outdoors, attach a 20-or 30-foot light line to puppy's collar to make sure he returns to you after a retrieve. The moment pup picks up the dummy, call him to you with a "Here" or "Come" command, and pop the line gently if he doesn't respond immediately. Run backwards as puppy is returning with the bumper, praising and calling his name excitedly to encourage a speedy return. Never run toward a puppy, especially if he's running the other way; he'll think it's a game of "Chase" and keep on going!

A cardinal rule of puppy training is to act wildly exuberant during training sessions to keep the puppy at peak excitement during this fundamental learning period. Most puppy owners get used to acting foolish to keep their puppies motivated. If you're not in

Puppy water retrieving lesson underway.

Kramer, Wylie, and Ginnie enjoy a water party on their first birthday!

good physical condition, puppy training will take its toll!

Once your puppy is reliable on his return, you can progress to using a helper or "gunner" to throw the bumper. Have that person stand in the field about 20 feet away, still on short cut grass so the bumper will be highly visible. Tell your pup to "Mark" and have the gunner shout "Hup, Hup" to attract the pup's attention. When the pup is focused on the thrower, give the gunner a signal (a nod of the head will do) to throw, again with more "Hups," then release the pup while the bumper is in mid-air. Use the same routine above for the pup's return.

If the puppy has trouble going all the way to the bumper, shorten the distance and don't increase it until he's having a regular measure of success. Two or three throws each session— no more.

Any retriever worth

his ducks should be a natural water dog. Whether your Golden splashes happily through puddles or tiptoes into the water, his introduction to swimming water should be a pleasant experience. A sudden plunge into icy water or an unexpected drop into water over a pup's head can leave a lasting and negative impression on a pup who might not be fond of the water to begin with.

Take your puppy to a shallow pond or beach area when both the weather and water temperature are warm and pleasant. Wade in with him, use lots of

Golden puppies bred by the author get their first taste of birds at five weeks old.

encouragement, toss a toy in running water (up to the dog's elbows), make it a game and keep it fun. Once he's running about with confidence, toss the toy a little farther each time to get him to extend his reach after each success. Don't push or scold, and stay near by to make him feel secure. Many puppies "puppy-paddle" at first, holding their heads high out of the water and splashing wildly with their front legs, while others take off swimming like old pros from their first attempt. Puppy paddlers eventually learn to keep their heads low and legs underwater—just be patient.

All field work is rooted in a solid foun-

dation of obedience training. A dog must have a sound set of basics in obedience in order to respond and be successful in the field. Your puppy must receive positive and consistent obedience training during its introduction to field work and beyond. His success in the field will depend on his ability to obey his owner or handler, and he can't do it without you.

Beyond this point, if you're serious about using your Golden in the field, you'll need a good book or two devoted to training a retriever puppy for field work. There are so many variables on this complex subject that any attempt to go further into the subject would be an injustice to the reader. If you have a Golden puppy who's wild to retrieve, haunt your local pet shop and book stores, research gun dog magazines, or get book references from your breeder. A solid foundation of good basic training will assure you of years of Golden pleasure in the field.

If you have a Golden puppy that is a retrieve-a-holic, read books on retriever puppy training and talk to field enthusiasts so you can train your puppy properly.

Should You Adopt an Adult Golden?

Puppies aren't for everyone. Just because you love puppies doesn't mean you could properly raise one or should add one to your household. If you have an erratic schedule or demanding business and family obligations, it could interfere with the time and energy you will need to raise a puppy who will require your constant attention. The puppy's needs are paramount for at least the first year of puppy's life and persist to some degree throughout his entire lifetime.

The author's Goldens: Arrow, Ginnie, China, Apache, and Quincy pose for a family portrait.

A well-behaved Golden is a joy to own. Ruggles awaits his Christmas gifts from mom and dad, Bob and Taimi Anderson.

But that doesn't mean you can't enjoy life with a Golden Retriever. An adult or older Golden who is housebroken and understands basic household manners could be a perfect candidate for the family who can't raise or train a pup.

Adult Goldens become available for a variety of reasons, reasons sometimes beyond the owner's control, and unfortunately often due to lack of foresight, patience or compassion... "the dog costs too much, jumps up on the kids, sheds, barks, digs, chews, etc."

Occasionally a breeder keeps a dog for several months or longer to evaluate its future in the field or show ring, then decides to place it in a pet home. There's nothing wrong with the pup...it simply didn't grow up to fulfill the breeder's expectations. In some cases a dog is retired in mid-life from its field or show career, or a bitch retired from breeding. These dogs may be under a year old or well into adulthood. But if the dog has been loved and well cared for, he is capable at any age of bonding to and loving any human being who offers him affection and attention. The typical Golden will easily adapt to a new environment if his new family is patient and caring and consistently reassures him he's in a safe and happy place.

As with a puppy, if you acquire an adult Golden, bring him home during a time when you can spend several days with the dog. Those first few days in a new and strange environment are very stressful for any dog, regardless of its age, and your constant presence and attention will help relieve his fears and apprehension. Give him a full tour of his new house and

Chances R Mein Leibschen CDX, WC, TDI owned by the author.

You should know the personality of an adult Golden to be sure it will get along with your other pets. This is Dusty lounging with a feline friend. Owner, Janet Edmonds.

to learn and understand what to expect and what will be expected of him.

You should also find out as much as possible about his former life and habits. The more you know about his past will help you understand why he has certain manners and behaviors, and you'll be better prepared to reorient him to life with you and your family.

Your new Golden will also have to learn you are now the alpha person in his life. The best way to establish that is through obedience training. Even a well-trained older dog will benefit from a formal class. An eager-to-please Golden loves to work and will

yard, and show him where he'll eat and sleep and potty. Don't assume he'll automatically know where to find his food bowl, bed or designated areas. Routine is important for canines. Your new dog will need enjoy the personal time and attention of a night out together and the training time spent in between. Obedience training after a reasonable adjustment period in his new home will help you and your dog better understand each other and become a team. Goldens are very intuitive to body language and other subtle signals. Training together will build your dog's confidence and trust in you as his new pack leader.

Handsome "Denver" is owned by Bob Green.

Rescue Goldens: Who Are They?

"Rescue" dogs, Golden Retrievers as well as members of every registered breed, are an unfortunate fact of the modern dog world. In a society soft on commitment and big on instant gratification, dogs are inevitable victims of today's throwaway mentality.

In 1990, over 18 million dogs and cats were euthanized at

No matter what breed of dog you choose, you are committing to the entire lifetime of the dog. Rescue Golden Sam (front) relaxes with his foster-sister Blaze.

One-year-old "Buddy" was found running loose in an airport field. His new adopted family adores him.

humane societies and animal shelters: an estimated 25 percent of those dogs were pure-bred castoffs, picked up as strays or re-leased to shelters or breed rescue volun-teers because they were no longer wanted. High-profile breeds like the Golden Retriever claim the most vic-tims... overpopulation is the end product of popularity.

Puppies-for-profit and backyard breeding will always produce potential cast-off dogs afflicted with heredi-tary problems— Goldens with hip dys-plasia, epilepsy and heart disease or Goldens who are people and dog-aggres-sive and no longer resemble the sweet-tempered and talented animal the Golden Retriever should be. However, the majority of stray and abandoned Goldens are victims of the human condition, dumped by selfish and uncaring owners who discard their dogs for reasons beyond a dog lover's comprehension: Too big, too rowdy, too untrained (certainly not the dog's fault). Not reasons, really, merely inconveniences.

Many Goldens are turned over to Rescue groups because the owner "has no time for him." Pretty Rusty now has a new home.

Breed rescue people intercede on behalf of these canine cast-offs. Rescue committees are made up of dedicated dog lovers who work with shelters, veterinarians and individual dog owners to provide foster and permanent homes for homeless and abandoned dogs of their particular breed. In 1994 the Golden Retriever Club of America had over 35 Golden Rescue services across the United States, most of those services affiliated with local member Golden Retriever clubs.

Rescue committees can relate horror stories by the hour about dozens, sometimes hundreds, of dogs starved and living in indescribable conditions, often amidst dogs dead of starvation and abuse. And despite Rescue's superhuman efforts, many rescued Goldens are unadoptable and must be euthanized because of irreversible health or behavior problems.

Yet many are saved, adopted by loving families willing to devote time and effort to rehabilitate these victims of canine inhumanity.

Not all rescue Goldens bear such tragic scars. Some

Tahoe was adopted by Becky Hayden at ten years old. At 15 she still rules the roost.

Goldens are turned over to Rescue by loving owners due to unexpected job or family changes. Many are stable, typical Goldens needing only a human to love and live for.

Rescue Golden Redford, found in an abandoned barn, was adopted by Donna Di Dio and is now "King of the House. It's like we've been together since he was a pup, people can't believe how well we fit. I waited a lifetime for this dog. Getting a Rescue Golden was the best thing I ever did."

Like the older Golden, Rescue is another alternative resource if you can't add a puppy to your family. Ask the owners of Rescue Goldens, and they'll answer in a single voice, "It's the best thing we ever did...go for it!"

The Senior Golden

No doubt about it... senior dogs are special friends.

Whether your senior Golden has been with you since puppyhood or was adopted as an older dog, you should be aware that old timers have special needs that differ from those of a pup or middle-age dog.

The average Golden lives for 10 to 13 years, although some still romp about (slowly, of course) and enjoy a quality life at 14 and 15. Like many humans,

The average Golden lives for 10 to 13 years. These three adults are Gopher, Daisey and Player owned by Dan and Ann Graham.

Just like humans, most Goldens turn gray or white as they age, but rarely lose their desire to play!

It is often said that one year of a dog's life equals seven of a human, but that's not entirely accurate. Puppies develop rapidly during their first two years, far surpassing the relative development of the equivalent seven-year-old child. A more realistic age comparison was developed by a French veterinarian. It compares canines and humans according to the following scale.

Dog's Age	Human Age
1 year	15 years
2 years	24 years
3 years	28 years
4 years	32 years
8 years	48 years
12 years	64 years
15 years	76 years
20 years	96 years

most Goldens turn gray or white with advanced age. And there are always a few mid-lifers who start to gray while still in their prime, with muzzles and eyebrows sprouting white streaks at five and six years of age.

As you can see, after the first two years of life, the dog's aging process slows down to four years of dog age for every human year. So the 10-year-old dog is not like a 70-year-old person as many would believe, but rather closer to a 56-year-old, which is a more optimistic per-spective for our older dogs.

Nutritional needs also change as a dog moves beyond middle-age. Veterinary nutritionists have researched canine dietary needs and found that a correct diet can greatly en-hance the quality and duration of life in the

This snowy senior is "Goldie" owned and treasured by Francis and Bernice Biegen.

Your senior Golden will not be as agile as when he was a pup. Goldie's owners, Francis and Bernice Biegen, shoveled a path through the yard for her during a winter storm.

progress of the latter two and may play an important role in cancer prevention as well.

Professional dietary guidelines suggest that our dogs fall into the "aging" category at about seven years old. In dietary terms more is definitely not better for the aging dog, and most veterinarians believe an older dog will remain healthier longer if he is fed a lower protein food. The protein in a dog food directly affects the kidneys, with kidney failure leading the pack as a major cause of death in older dogs. The kidneys function as a metabolic clearinghouse for dietary waste products. More protein, more waste, which means more

older dog. The three most common causes of canine death are cancer, heart disease and kidney disease. Diet has proven to significantly reduce the development and work for the aging kidneys of the older dog.

So in dietary terms, less is better for dogs over seven or eight years old. That doesn't mean a lower quality food, rather the same high-quality food with the protein level reduced to 14 to 16 percent. Older dogs also tend to be less active, which means they require fewer calories, about 40 percent less than younger dogs. You can maintain your senior dog's normal feeding routine and simply change from a "performance" or "maintenance" food to a "senior" food and if necessary, reduce the amount of food you give.

Reduced protein will also control the onset or progression of obesity. Obesity puts a strain on all vital organs, especially the heart and lungs, and simply put, an overweight dog will live a shorter life. Thus

This is Magnum, owned and adored by the Speciale family. A senior Golden should visit the vet more frequently during his sunset years.

Twelve-year-old Josie with her "baby brother" Max. Max gave Josie a renewed interest in life, and she's up and about again despite severe arthritis. Owners, Bob and Nancy Pellegrino.

preserving his lithe and limber figure is healthy as well as handsome!

Though many Goldens remain active and enthusiastic well past nine or even ten years of age, their bodies and reflexes tend to slow down with age. Be sure to encourage moderate exercise in your senior dog. Adequate physical activity is important to maintain healthy muscle tone and circulation. A physically fit dog will stay younger and healthier longer than his overweight, couch-cushion counterpart. It's also more difficult for the older dog to "catch up" on an exercise routine after he's been sedentary for a long period of time.

Regular physical activity and proper diet will also keep an old dog's bowels moving in a healthy fashion. The bowels also lose muscle tone with age, which can lead to constipation. You can help regulate the bowels by adding bran cereals or fiber granules to the diet if your older dog has difficulty passing stools.

Older dogs sometimes tend to have more flatulence. If yours is affected, try to

Chances R Rusty at 15+ years owned, loved and missed by Debbie Stremke.

At 14 years old, "Pretty Lady," or Brandy, is much loved by the John Gibbs family though doesn't play piano as much these years.

avoid foods and milk products that can contribute to the passing of wind *and* be patient and long suffering!

Urinary dribbling is a common problem in older spayed bitches. This usually comes as a surprise to the dog as well as the owner. Fortunately it can be treated with a hormone supplement that improves the muscle tone of the weakened sphincter muscle in the bladder.

As with aging humans, older dogs experience changes in their sensory perceptions. Their faculties dwindle, they don't see or hear as well as they used to, and they sleep longer and more deeply than before. Many older dogs go deaf or develop the cloudy eye lens associated with aging, but fortunately they cope very well at home with these conditions. Be careful with a deaf or vision-impaired dog outdoors, however. He can easily wander into the street and become a victim of a passing car.

Other changes may arise with age, although these do not occur the same extent in all dogs. Recognizing these changes may help you understand some of your old dog's mood swings.

His taste perception may change, which can result in loss of appetite. Try warming his food to increase palatability. The sense of smell can also deteriorate, which may be linked to loss of taste. Many older dogs experience a decreased ability to regulate their body temperature and may be less tolerant of heat or cold.

As the owner of a senior dog, you should know the warning signs that could indicate heart or kidney problems in your dog.

Heart disease, if recognized early, can be treated effectively to minimize the dog's

Chances R Gingersnap rules the Pertle Household with a gentle paw.

distress. Symptoms include coughing, especially at night or upon first awaking in the morning, a decreased tolerance for exercise, fluid build-up in the abdomen, excessive panting and listlessness.

The warning signs of kidney malfunction may include excessive thirst and more frequent urination, weight loss, listlessness and vomiting. Your veterinarian can perform a urinalysis and other tests to determine if the kidneys are working properly.

Semi-annual visits to your veterinarian will focus on early detection of treatable conditions. Your vet can tailor a program to control age-related behavior problems or hormonal imbalances.

Older Goldens will slow down but still love to romp in the snow or play with toys.

A senior dog will still enjoy a trip to the shore. Magnum still fetches sticks at 12 years old.

Routine vaccinations and parasite control are even more life enhancing for an older pet with a decreasing ability to rebound from illness or disease.

On the plus side, an old dog learns to appreciate life in the slow lane. He asks little of his human other than a soft touch or a bit of treat. His pleasures are simple, and he is usually happy napping in the sun or curled up at your feet in front of the TV. His very presence warms you with a passing parade of happy memories.

Yet despite our efforts to preserve our dog's youth and keep him with us "forever,"

Chances R Milady, "Mollie," still loved to retrieve even in her "Golden" years. Owned by the author.

the time will come to say good-bye. The dog who suffers from cancer or another terminal disease will look to his owner for relief from constant pain or inability to function. Your dog deserves your help when that time arrives.

If you face such a decision, your vet will advise you on the how and when. Euthanasia is probably the most difficult decision of dog ownership and possibly the most unselfish. Many owners elect to remain with their dogs to hold and comfort them while the vet performs this last ministration. If you are unable or unwilling to attend the dog, a friend or family member might serve in your stead. Your faithful companion should not die alone.

Responsibilities as a Golden Owner

Dogs arrive at breed Rescue because of irresponsible dog breeders and owners. Your job as the proud owner of a Golden Retriever is to become the opposite, a responsible, knowledgeable and caring dog owner whose Golden will thrive under your care.

Responsibility means confining your dog. The neighborhood is not your dog's backyard. No dog should ever be allowed to

Baby gates help to confine puppies and dogs to certain areas of the house.

Start teaching your Golden pup to walk on a leash at a very early age.

often into the path of a car or truck. Most reputable breeders refuse to sell a puppy to a home without a fenced yard or chainlink dog run. Unconfined dogs end up stolen, hit by cars, caught in animal traps, poisoned by varmint bait or rotting garbage, or pregnant by a roaming suitor. Don't let that happen to your precious Golden.

Responsible dog owners own and use a leash...it's your dog's safety net and lifeline. The sight of it in your hands should throw him into a frenzy of excitement, thinking about a walk with Mom or Dad, obedience training, or going somewhere fun. A leash also means

roam free, run loose or exercise off-lead in unfenced areas. Even the best trained dog will succumb to its natural instincts and chase a rabbit, cat or squirrel at full speed, protection and control...protection from injury to a pet who might dart out into traffic, birth control by preventing unsupervised roaming and possible random matings and unwanted puppies. A leash is an automatic good neighbor policy, keeping your pet off lawns and from jumping on children and strangers. It means safety from stray dogs or animals who might entice an unleashed pet into a chase or fight. It's your pet's guarantee of your affection, as the touch of it assures him he is loved and protected.

The dog-end of the leash, his collar, should carry a tag or riveted plate bearing your name, address and telephone number for identification should the dog become lost. Don't include the dog's name; it will enable a thief to call the dog by name and possibly claim him. Some ID tags state "Reward offered," "Dog tattooed," or "Dog

When outdoors, be sure your Golden has fresh water available, especially in hot weather.

Rescue Golden Sam, owned by Lance Hollwig, lounges on his own pillow. Lance says Sam is a best friend to the entire family.

needs medication" to discourage potential theft and encourage a compassionate individual to return the dog. The collar should also carry any required local dog license and rabies tag. These can be traced by animal control and could save a lost pet from euthanasia. Proper identification is security.

The most permanent form of identification is a tattoo.

Dogs over six months of age can be tattooed on the inside of their thigh. The process is quick and painless. You can use your social security number or the dog's AKC registration number, then register the tattoo with the National Dog Registry.

Animal shelters and veterinarians will call the registry for owner identification whenever a tattooed animal is brought in.

The microchip is another permanent method of dog identification, one that has gained enormous acceptance and popularity since its introduction in the early 1990s. The microchip is encoded with a series of permanent characters that identify the dog for his lifetime. Encapsulated in the same type of glass used in human prosthetic devices, and about the size of a grain of rice, the chip is injected into the soft

An exercise pen is a great way to confine your Golden Retriever to a safe area. It is especially handy while traveling with your pet. Never leave a confined animal unsupervised.

tissue between the dog's shoulder blades and will not migrate from that site. The injection procedure is completely painless and will not harm the dog. Microchip implantation must be done by a veterinarian or other trained professional.

In 1995 AKC also ventured into the world of microchip identification. They joined forces with Schering-Plough

A new method of identification is microchipping. The microchip is a computer chip no bigger than a grain of rice that is implanted in the dog as a means of permanent identification.

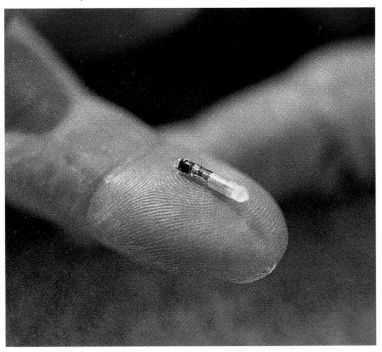

A collar tag is one important means of identifying your Golden should it get lost. These tagged dogs are Cogan and Courage owned by Ron Buksaitis.

Pharmaceutical Company to launch the "Home Again" program which offers a nationwide database management service for microchip identification. An animal implanted with the Schering-Plough Destron microchip is automatically enrolled in the "Home Again" program. As the database manager, AKC provides a 24-hour-a-day, 800-number recovery service for any animal thus identified.

It may be that a tattoo *and* a microchip would give your dog the best protection. After all, you can't be too careful with your best friend!

As a responsible dog owner, you should train your Golden to become a good neighbor. A well-trained dog is a welcome member of any community—it sends an important message that dogs can be good citizens too, setting an example for others to follow. A good-neighbor dog is also a valuable tool in fighting potential anti-canine legislation, which could ultimately affect your right to own and live with a dog.

To promote that end as well as respond to the growing anti-canine sentiment in society today, in 1989 the AKC launched the Canine Good Citizen program. Mixed breeds are eligible to participate (at non-AKC events) since the anti-dog population doesn't discriminate between the pure-bred and non-pure-bred dog.

CGC tests are designed to demonstrate that the dog, as a companion of man, can be a respected member of the community. To demonstrate confidence and control, the dog must complete the ten steps have been determined by AKC. Local dog obedience and kennel clubs conduct CGC classes and administer the tests, and dogs who qualify

Goldens love Christmas too! Altair's Tara Marie and Jessie visit Santa Claus. Owner, Maria Zoul.

A crate will provide your Golden with his own safe place when traveling.

are awarded the official CGC title from AKC. This is a title every responsible Golden owner and his dog should aspire to and earn.

Provide a safe and loving environment for your Golden. As with a toddler (and your dog will be that equivalent all his life), be con-

scious of the dangers in everyday life that might harm your dog. Heatstroke...on a breezy summer day, a car with windows partially open can still heat to over 120 degrees in minutes... heavy exercise on hot, humid days... unshaded kennel runs...don't put your dog at risk.

Never allow your dog to ride loose in the back of a pick-up truck. Statistics show that thousands of dogs die every year because they were bounced around, thrown from or jumped out of moving pick-up trucks. It is illegal in many states and an invitation to disaster anywhere it occurs.

Learn everything you can about Golden Retrievers and canine care. An educated and well-informed owner has a healthier and better behaved companion. Don't ever assume the attitude, "dogs will be dogs."

Spay or neuter your Golden so you will not contribute to the overpopulation of this gentle breed. Breeding a Golden for the wrong reasons would be a disservice to the breed and to the potential buyers of the resulting pups; simply loving your dog will not automatically make you a knowledgeable or responsible dog breeder. Almost every good breeder knows at least one well-intentioned dog owner who bred their dog haphazardly because:

1. Their dog is beautiful, smart, great with kids, sweetheart disposition, etc. They knew a handsome dog down the street or one owned by a friend or a friend's friend, and

A well-behaved Golden is an asset to his owner and community.

Much time and energy goes into raising a litter of puppies. This Goldenbear puppy has definitely outgrown his food pan.

thought they would have beautiful puppies together.

"Beautiful" isn't enough. Is your bitch (or male) an excellent representative of the breed with a superb pedigree behind her? Is she structurally sound and her temperament truly "Golden?" Has she been tested and found free of hereditary defects such as hip dysplasia, eye defects,

heart and blood disease? Few inexperienced Golden owners can properly assess their dog for breeding potential.

2. A litter of pups would be an educational experience for the children...one puppy born is supposed to be worth the perennial thousand words.

Whelping a litter of pups is far from child's play. Your dog might require a Cesarean delivery, even die from complications in a normal whelping. Puppies die unexpectedly. Raising and socializing the entire litter are work, not fun, and are beyond a child's comprehension.

3. Having puppies will calm the dog and

fulfill her natural instincts.

A bitch has no desire to deliver pups, her only instinct is to mate. Pregnancy will not alter her temperament or calm her down, nor will it affect or improve her health in any way.

4. They want a puppy from their own sweet dog.

What will you do with the other 10 or 12 puppies in the litter? It would be easier and wiser to get another pup from your dog's breeder, or from a breeder who may own a littermate to your dog. There's also no guarantee the puppy you keep will inherit its mother's lovely qualities. Pups combine the genes of both

Keeping order among a six-week-old litter is nearly impossible. After eating, it takes only seconds for 12 puppies to turn their playroom into a disaster zone. Who says breeding dogs is fun!?

Puppies need to be with their littermates for their first seven weeks to learn proper canine etiquette.

parents as well as other ancestors. Even experienced breeders can't duplicate their best specimens.

5. Selling pups is a good way to make extra money.

Far from it. The stud fee, veterinary expenses, feeding the dam and her puppies, advertising, routine and emergency care generally exceed any monies from puppy sales. Your bitch might need an expensive Cesarean delivery or have a litter of 10 or 12, and you could be stuck with unsold pups for several weeks. She could die from complications during labor or delivery.

Screening buyers, placing puppies in good homes, and educating the new owners on quality animal care are time consuming and exhausting. Few novice dog owners have the knowledge, time, facilities or money required to properly raise and place or sell a litter of puppies.

There are also many health benefits from spaying and neutering. Your dog will live a longer life and it won't ever miss having that litter of pups. Neither will you.

Brumley relaxes with his favorite music on his headset. Owners, Tom and DeeDee Moore.

All Goldens should be trained to be well-mannered members of the community.

TRAINING YOUR DOG TO BE A CANINE GOOD CITIZEN

The ten steps of the CGC Test:

1. *Accepting a Friendly Stranger:* This test demonstrates that the dog will allow a friendly stranger to approach it and speak to the handler in a natural everyday situation. The evaluator and handler shake hands and exchange

pleasantries. The dog must show no sign of resentment or shyness and must not break position or try to go to the evaluator.

2. *Sitting Politely for Petting:* This test demonstrates that the dog will allow a friendly stranger to touch it while it is out with its handler. The evaluator pets the dog then circles the dog and handler. The dog must not show shyness or resentment.

3. *Appearance and Grooming:* This practical test demonstrates that the dog will welcome being groomed and examined and will permit a stranger to do so. It also demonstrates the owner's care, concern and responsibility. The

evaluator inspects the dog, then combs or brushes the dog and lightly examines the ear and each front foot.

4. *Out for a Walk (Walking on a Loose Leash):* This test demonstrates that the handler is in proper

This is Eileen Robinson training her Golden Retriever Thornfield's Mister Mario CD for the sit/stay.

Littermates Kramer, Wylie, Jennie and Ginnie perform a sit-stay on their first birthday party.

control of the dog. The evaluator must use a pre-plotted course or may direct the handler and dog by issuing instructions and commands. There must be a left turn, a right turn and an about turn, with at least one stop in between and another at the end. The dog need not be perfectly aligned with the handler and need not sit when the handler stops.

5. *Walk through a Crowd:* This test demonstrates that the dog can move about politely in pedestrian

Dog shows are fun events that dogs and their owners can enjoy together. Goldens are among the most popular participants in conformation shows.

Thornfield's Mister Mario CD demonstrates the down on command with Eileen Robinson.

interest in the strangers.

6. *Sit and Down on Command/Staying in Place:* This test demonstrates that the dog has training, will respond to the handler's command to sit and down will remain in place when commanded by the handler (sit or down position, whichever the handler prefers). The handler may take a reasonable amount of time and use more than one command.

7. *Coming When Called:* This test demonstrates the dog will come when called by the handler. The handler will walk ten feet from the dog, turn to face the dog and then call the dog. Handlers may tell the dog to "stay" or "wait" or they

traffic and is under control in public places. The dog and handler walk around and pass close to several people. The dog may show some may simply walk away. The dog may be left in the sit, down or standing position. The handler may use body language or encour-agement when calling the dog.

8. *Reactions to Another Dog:* This test demonstrates that the dog can behave politely

"Dasty," a lovely Golden imported from Sweden by Alice Landin, is very attentive.

This is Thundering Dakota in repose, owned and loved by Kevin Kilgore.

around other dogs. Two handlers and their dogs approach each other from a distance of about ten yards, stop, shake hands or exchange pleasantries, and continue on for about five yards. The dogs should show no more than a casual interest in each other.

9. *Reactions to Distractions:* This test demonstrates that the

dog is confident at all times when faced with common distracting situations. The dog may express a natural interest and curiosity and may appear slightly startled, but should not panic, try to run away, show aggressiveness or bark.

10. *Supervised Separation:* This test demonstrates that the dog can be left with another person while the owner goes out of sight. The dog will be attached to a six-foot line (the dog's leash). The dog does not have to stay in position but should not bark, whine, howl, pace unnecessarily or show anything other than mild agitation or ner-vousness.

The CGC test is

This Golden Retriever is practicing the down/stay with trainer Dorman Pantfoeder.

Kirby earned her Canine Good Citizen award at six months of age! Owner, Debbie Stremke.

always under review by AKC, and some minor changes will occur from time to time. The goal is always the same...to establish the dog as a well-mannered and respectful member of the community. Before performing these requirements, the dog's owner must present a current rabies certificate and other locally required inoculation certificates and license.

Your Dog's Body Signs

Temperature: 100.5 to 101.5°F. Taken rectally. Heat or activity may raise it by one or two degrees. To take your dog's temperature, dip the bulb of the thermometer in petroleum jelly and insert it into the rectum with a firm, gentle rotary action. If you

You should be familiar with your dog's body language to monitor his health. This is "Gopher" owned by Dan and Ann Graham.

Discuss any sudden or extreme changes in your Golden's temperament or behavior with your veterinarian.

strike a fecal mass, try again. Leave in a full three minutes. The new "instant" thermometers are great for this!

Heart: At rest, the normal canine heart rate averages 90 to 100 beats per minute.

Faster in puppies and older dogs. A resting dog's heart normally has an irregular beat, faster on inhalation, slower on expiration. The heartbeat can be felt through the chest wall just behind the flex of the front leg. Also on the inner side of the hind leg.

Respiration: The normal rate of respiration is between 18 to 28 breaths per minute. Rapid or mouth breathing while at rest may indicate trouble.

Eyes: The white on top half of the eye should be bright and clear with a few small vessels. The lower half of the eyelid should be a bright healthy pink. The cornea (clear part) should be glistening and clear. Accumulated matter can be removed with a moistened cotton swab or damp tissue.

Ears: Inside the ear folds should be smooth, pink and the ear canal should be clean. Dust and dirt may collect in the folds. To clean ears, use a cotton swab dipped in alcohol. Do not put oily substances into the ear, as that will hold moisture and cause more problems. A brownish waxy substance, a foul odor or inflammation indicates mites or an infection.

Nose: A Golden's nose should be black and smooth, may turn brown or pinkish in cold weather. Moist, dry or cold has little to do with the dog's temperature.

Teeth: Should be white and free of tartar and debris. Nylabones® help remove tartar. Never feed rawhide unsupervised to prevent choking from swallowing too large a chunk. Stories

Nylabones® are wonderful chew devices for your Golden Retriever. They help remove tartar and keep your dog's teeth in good condition.

abound about dogs who have died from choking on pieces of swallowed rawhide.

Gums: Should be bright, clear pink, and may be partially pigmented. Puppy gums may be slightly paler.

Tongue: Bright pink and clean, pigmented areas or black spots are normal.

Paws: Nails must be trimmed if they are not worn down on outdoor concrete. In light-colored nails the quick is seen as a pink or darker line. Trim just in front of the quick. A flashlight held under the nail will help define the quick, especially helpful on dark or black nails. Use a styptic or other coagulant to stop accidental bleeding if a quick is nipped. You can also poke the nail into a bar of soap.

Nylabone® products help to satisfy your Golden's chewing needs as well as promote good dental hygiene and better breath.

Your Golden Retriever will be your best friend for a great many years. It is your responsibility to keep him in the best possible health. "Dreamer" at six weeks, owned by Brian and Lisa Hartfield.

Index

Suggested Reading

The World of the
Golden Retriever
By Nona Kilgore Bauer
A DOG FOR ALL SEASONS
The World of the
Golden Retriever:

**The World of the
Golden Retriever**

by Nona Kilgore Bauer

TS-197

The author's first book on the Golden Retriever won the Dog Writers of America's highest award for Breed Book of the Year. *The World of the Golden Retriever* spans 480 pages and is illustrated by over 700 spectacular full-color photographs. Nona Bauer presents this "Dog for All Seasons" as the most versatile and heartwarming dog of all. Included are the history, standard, GRCA national specialty, showing, obedience, field trials, service dogs, therapy dogs, search and detection dogs, selection, health, and overviews of Goldens in Canada, England, Australia, Europe, and more. Guest authors include Marcia Schier, Betty Gay, Chris Walkowicz, Jean Dodds, DVM, Lucille Sawtell and Barbara Goodman. By far, *The World of the Golden Retriever* is the most beautiful and comprehensive volume ever published on this delightful "Golden" companion.